Knowing the Real

Toronto Studies in Religion

Donald Wiebe
General Editor

Vol. 20

PETER LANG
New York • Washington, D.C./Baltimore
Bern • Frankfurt am Main • Berlin • Vienna • Paris

Kenneth Rose

Knowing the Real

John Hick on the Cognitivity of Religions and Religious Pluralism

PETER LANG
New York • Washington, D.C./Baltimore
Bern • Frankfurt am Main • Berlin • Vienna • Paris

Library of Congress Cataloging-in-Publication Data

Rose, Kenneth.
Knowing the real: John Hick on the cognitivity
of religions and religious pluralism/ Kenneth Rose.
p. cm. — (Toronto studies in religion; vol. 20)
Includes bibliographical references and index.
1. Hick, John. 2. Religion—Philosophy. 3. Religious pluralism.
4. Christianity and other religions. I. Title. II. Series.
BL43.H53R67 210'.92—dc20 94-23673
ISBN 0-8204-2636-9
ISSN 8756-7385

Die Deutsche Bibliothek-CIP-Einheitsaufnahme

Rose, Kenneth:
Knowing the real: John Hick on the cognitivity of religions and religious
pluralism/ Kenneth Rose. –New York; Washington, D.C./Baltimore; Bern;
Frankfurt am Main; Berlin; Vienna; Paris: Lang.
(Toronto studies in religion; Vol. 20)
ISBN 0-8204-2636-9
NE: GT

The paper in this book meets the guidelines for permanence and durability
of the Committee on Production Guidelines for Book Longevity
of the Council of Library Resources.

© 1996 Peter Lang Publishing, Inc., New York

Printed in the United States of America.

To My Mother,
Ellen Cole Rose
and
the Memory of my Father,
Lester ("Jim Parker") Rose

The Truth must dazzle gradually
Or every man be blind.
                                    —Emily Dickinson
                                    "Tell All the Truth"

Acknowledgments

First of all, I want to express my appreciation to Gordon D. Kaufman for his careful overseeing of this work from its inception, as well as for his direction during my years in the M.Div. and Ph.D. programs at Harvard University. He sets a high standard for theological writing from which he would not let me stray. Appreciation is also due to Hilary Putnam for his support and helpful criticism throughout the writing of this book. He saved me from more than a few philosophical slips along the way. I also want to acknowledge Francis Schüssler Fiorenza for suggesting that I consider writing on John Hick as a way of combining my interests in philosophy, theology, and world religions.

I would like to thank John Hick for a helpful discussion of his writings and my interpretation of his views over lunch in Kansas City during the 1991 meeting of the American Academy of Religion.

Hearty thanks to Diana Eck, who garnered funding for final year dissertation students from the Mellon Foundation. As a recipient of one of these fellowships, I am grateful to Professor Eck and the Mellon Foundation for enabling me to finish my dissertation in a much shorter time than would otherwise have been possible.

I want to express my gratitude to John and Ineke Carman. Their various kindnesses, great and small, during the seven years that I lived in the stimulating environment of the Center for the Study of World Religions at Harvard University eased my passage through graduate school. At the Center, I want particularly to single out Narges Moshiri, whose gentle spirit and selfless dedication continues the tradition of the Carmans at the Center.

First among numerous intellectual comrades and fellow inhabitants of the graduate student trenches at Harvard and at the Center were Adina Davidovich and Ehud Benor, to whom I express my warmest regards. Their friendship and encouragement urged and cheered me on during years of strenuous effort. I will also remember fondly the fun, debates, and sharing of rites of passage with many other friends from my years at the Center, particularly Steven and Adrienne Caddell Hopkins, Harriet Crabtree, Irit Auerbuch, and Brian and Alison Hatcher. Also, not to be forgotten is the late and lamented Little Dickens.

For encouraging me to bring this book to press, thanks to my editor, Dr. Heidi Burns, of Peter Lang Publishing, Inc. For technical assistance, thanks also to Lisa Dillon, Production Manager at Peter Lang.

For incisive and suggestive discussions of the issues raised in this book, I am indebted to Prof. Robison James, Department of Religion, University of Richmond, Richmond, Virginia.

For supporting the publication of this book, thanks to Jouett Powell, Acting Provost of Christopher Newport University, Newport News, Virginia. For bibliographical assistance during the final stage of the preparation of this book, thanks are due also to librarian Catherine Doyle of the Captain John Smith Library, Christopher Newport University.

For kind permission to quote from John Hick, *The Interpretation of Religion: Human Responses to the Transcendent*, grateful acknowledgment is made to Yale University Press.

I want especially to thank my mother, Ellen Rose, for her steadfast example of courage and charity; my late father, Lester Rose, for his brilliant humor and a dreaming illumined by starlight; and skydancer Miranda Shaw, peerless companion, for better or for better.

Contents

Abbreviations

CC	*Christianity at the Centre.* New York: Herder and Herder, 1970.
DEL	*Death and Eternal Life.* New York: Harper and Row, 1976.
EG	*The Existence of God,* John Hick, ed. New York: Macmillan, 1964.
FK1	*Faith and Knowledge: A Modern Introduction to the Problem of Religious Knowledge.* Ithaca: Cornell University Press, 1957.
FK2	*Faith and Knowledge,* 2d ed. 1966; reprint, London: Macmillan, 1988.
FP	*Faith and the Philosophers.* London: Macmillan, 1964.
GHMNUK	*God Has Many Names.* London: Macmillan, 1980.
GHMNUS	*God Has Many Names.* Philadelphia: The Westminster Press, 1982.
GUF	*God and the Universe of Faiths,* 2d ed. 1977; reprint, London: Macmillan, 1988.
IR	*An Interpretation of Religion: Human Responses to the Transcendent.* Yale University Press, 1989.
MCU	*The Myth of Christian Uniqueness: Toward a Pluralistic Theology of Religions,* John Hick and Paul Knitter, eds. Maryknoll, NY: Orbis Books, 1987.
MGI	*The Myth of God Incarnate,* John Hick, ed. Philadelphia: The Westminster Press, 1977.
PR1	*Philosophy of Religion,* 1st ed. Englewood Cliffs, NJ: Prentice-Hall, 1963.
PR2	*Philosophy of Religion,* 2nd ed. Englewood Cliffs, NJ: Prentice-Hall, 1973.
PRP	*Problems of Religious Pluralism* London: Macmillan, 1985.
WBG	Michael Goulder and John Hick, *Why Believe in God?* London: SCM Press, 1983.

1

Introduction

Of all the issues facing theology, philosophy of religion, and religious studies at the end of the millennium, one of the most pressing is that of religious pluralism. With the collapse of the enforced centralism and stability of the Communist regimes in Eastern Europe has come the tragedy of civil conflict fired by ethnic, linguistic, and religious differences, as in the former Yugoslavia. Orthodox Serbians, Bosnian Muslims, and Roman Catholic Croats, longtime neighbors in ancient villages, have set upon each other murderously for the sake of ethnic and religious purification. A fearsome phrase has thus been added to our language: *ethnic cleansing*.

Owing to the protections guaranteed under the First Amendment to the U.S. Constitution, religion has more or less been neutralized as a source of civil—though not political—conflict in this country. Yet in too many parts of the world no such détente between religion and society has been achieved. A short and incomplete list of countries and regions where violence has been spawned in part by religious differences would include: Sri Lanka, India, Nigeria, Northern Ireland, the Middle East, and the Balkans. In each of these conflicts, religious differences and the misunderstanding and mistrust that these differences foster have been the occasion for the deployment of weaponry and the shedding of blood. Given the brutality and apparent irrationality of such religious violence, it is necessary to find ways of negotiating religious differences without underplaying these differences, yet also without allowing them to become justifications for civil war.

Religion is not about to disappear, nor are religious differences. However, if the history of religion in the United States—a land of a bewildering diversity of religious opinion—may be taken as a guide and as a source of hope, it is entirely possible that a nonviolent way of mediating the volatile energies of religious exclusivism and absolutism may be achieved and sustained.

Despite the progress that has been made since Vatican II within Protestant and Roman Catholic circles on religious pluralism, religious exclusivism and absolutism seem to have grown more influential. This can be seen in the rise all over the globe in the last decade or so of militant antimodernistic movements within the major religious traditions. No longer does the term *fundamentalism* signify only a variety of evangelical Protestant religion centered in North America. The term has been expanded, not without controversy, to cover a heterogeneous assortment of movements of Islāmic, Jewish, Buddhist, Hindu, Roman Catholic, and Protestant provenance.

Academic interest in generating relatively unbiased accounts of these fundamentalist insurgencies is finding expression in the various productions of the Fundamentalism Project, a venture sponsored by the American Academy of Sciences and guided by the religious historian Martin E. Marty. While it may be interesting to learn about various fundamentalisms, the most important use of the information gathered by the Fundamentalism Project ought to be to help blunt or soften the absolutism and exclusivism that animate these movements. This goal, however, cannot be achieved simply through phenomenological and historical studies of these religious movements, as important as such studies are. Besides accurate information, theological and philosophical criticism of claims to religious absolutism and exclusivism is necessary. The latter effort is one of the guiding purposes of this book.

Given this purpose, my choice of John Hick as the subject of this book should be obvious to those who are familiar with the development of his thought over the past four decades. For those less familiar with his writings, I will briefly suggest something of the character of this development.

Through encounter with students belonging to the Inter-Varsity Fellowship, Hick was exposed to a version of conservative evangelical/fundamentalist Protestantism while a law student in Hull, England. As a result of numerous discussions with these fellow students and through a reading of the New Testament, Hick felt strongly the influence of Jesus as lord and savior. This experience led Hick to experience

> a period of several days of intense mental and emotional turmoil during which I was powerfully aware of a higher truth and a greater reality pressing in upon my consciousness and claiming my recognition and response. At first this intrusion was highly unwelcome, a disturbing and challenging demand for nothing less than a revolution in personal identity. But presently the disturbing claim became a liberating invitation and I entered with great joy into the world of Christian faith (*GHMNUS*, 14–15).[1]

Although, as Hick writes, "at this stage I accepted as a whole and without question the entire evangelical package of theology" (*GHMNUS*, 15), he was not predisposed to do so. He could have gone the way of theosophy, a syncretistic sect that synthesizes central elements of Asian religions and philosophies and Western religious esotericism and mysticism. Some time earlier than his evangelical conversion, he came across a volume expounding theosophy

> and felt strongly the attraction of the first comprehensive and coherent interpretation of life that I had encountered. But although impressed, I was nevertheless not quite convinced by it, and, at a certain point I consciously rejected it as being too tidy and impersonal. Nevertheless I was in a state of spiritual searching. The Eastern religious world, in the form of theosophy, was attractive, but not sufficiently so for me to enter it. The

Western religious world of Christianity was all around me but seemed utterly lifeless and uninteresting (*GHMNUS*, 14).

One sees here a young person who might have gone either way: East or West. Given what he characterizes as the "infinite boredom" he felt at Anglican services as a child, he seems to have been a good bet to go with the novelty of a quasi-Eastern religious path. However, the "impersonal" aspect of the Westernized form of Hindu nondualism that he encountered in theosophy was at odds with a religious feeling that Hick says he has known almost since he can remember of God as "the personal loving lord of the universe, and of life as having a meaning within God's purpose" (*GHMNUS*, 14).

Certainly the personalistic piety and moralism of conservative evangelical religion are more fitted to nourish this feeling than religious nondualism, which tends toward impersonal or transpersonal conceptions of the divine. One wonders, however, what Hick's response would have been had he encountered the personalistic form of Hindu theism, *bhakti*, with its intense and emotionally rich devotion centered upon the Hindu deity Kṛṣṇa, that became popular for a time among the spiritually searching youth of the late sixties, particularly in the United States. His decision to become an evangelical Protestant may have been more difficult, as was often the case for many spiritually searching young persons in the religious fringe of the counterculture of the sixties who found themselves caught between the equally intense devotees of two very different but distinctly personal lords, Jesus and Kṛṣṇa.

Hick was spared this sort of dilemma, at least for a time. Theologically, he remained quite conservative until the mid-sixties, when, as an implication of the theodicy that he worked out in his now classic *Evil and the God of Love*, he had come to the unorthodox belief that "any viable Christian theodicy must affirm the ultimate salvation of all God's creatures" (*GHMNUS*, 17). At first this belief was merely an abstract implication of his evolving theology. As Hick himself writes, however, this abstraction took on a living urgency when, in 1967, he became a professor in the ethnically and racially diverse city of Birmingham, England, and for the first time encountered Muslim, Sikh, Hindu, and Jewish communities. He tells how, as a result of these encounters, he was

> drawn into the work which is variously called 'race relations' and 'community relations,' and soon had friends and colleagues in all these non-Christian religious communities as well as in the large black community from the Caribbean. And occasionally attending worship in mosque and synagogue, temple, and gurdwara, it was evident to me that essentially the same kind of thing is taking place in them as in a Christian church—namely, human beings opening their minds to a higher divine Reality (*GHMNUS*, 17–18).

He also came at this time under the influence of Wilfred Cantwell Smith and his view that religious traditions continually influence one another and are thus not isolated entities, of which one may assert of this one that it is true and of that one that it is false. Under the impetus of these influences, Hick called, in 1972, for a Copernican revolution in theology. Breaking quite thoroughly with orthodox theology of religions, even in the irenic, inclusivistic form that it took under the influence of Roman Catholic theologian Karl Rahner and of Vatican II,[2] Hick proposed to displace Christ from the center of the universe of faiths, replacing him with God. Having done so, Hick now viewed religions other than Christianity not as somehow aiming unconsciously at Jesus Christ but as independently valid human responses to the one divine Reality, which Hick, at this point, still called God (*GHMNUS*, 18–19).

Thus, from an orthodox defender of a high Christology—he felt compelled in an early article to attack the less than orthodox Christology of D. M. Baillie (*GHMNUS*, 15)—Hick became a proponent of a low Christology, one which would not be completely uncongenial to a theosophist (as exclusivistic, orthodox Christology certainly is). This shift in Hick's theology of religions and Christology brought him further prominence in the theological world and drew him into much controversy. It also led him to undertake the editorship of the controversial volume *The Myth of God Incarnate* (1977), to which he also contributed an article, entitled "Jesus and the World Religions." Those familiar with recent theology will likely remember the commotion both within and outside the theological world that was stirred by the appearance of this book.

Most important in this change in Hick's theology was not his new view of Christology but rather his attempt to rethink Christianity as an equal partner and not as the nisus, telos, or crisis,[3] acknowledged or not, of other religious traditions. In calling for a Copernican revolution in theology, Hick was decisively moving out of the mentality of religious absolutism and exclusivism.

After some years of attention to other topics—Christology and eschatology—Hick returned to the issue of religious pluralism. In response to Christian and Hindu critics of the theocentricity of the Copernican revolution in theology, Hick pushed beyond the theology of religions into the realm of the philosophy of religions. In so doing, he has once again made a distinctive contribution to the study of religions. In his philosophy of religions, Hick tries to avoid the extremes of perennialism, which reduces the many religions to dialectical variants of a universal esoteric wisdom, and of constructivism, which views the many religions as irreducibly different. In his 1986–87 Gifford Lectures, published as *An Interpretation of Religion: Human Responses to the Transcendent*, Hick seeks the middle path between these two views by holding in dialectical tension both the uniqueness and the commonality of the many religious traditions of the world. Thus we see Hick attempting, once again, to provide theorists of religions with a comprehensive, systematic view, one that may push the study of religions beyond the impasse of perennialism and constructivism. This innovative interpretation of religions is likely to stimulate further attempts to produce philosophies of religions, whether or not Hick's own proposal proves persuasive.

Another aim of this book is to provide support for the controversial belief that religions have an inalienable cognitive dimension. That is, religions, whether by way of stories or doctrines, present views or visions of life that are thought by those who orient their lives by them to be true. That religions speak veridically—though how they do so is nearly an impenetrable mystery—is one of the most basic convictions guiding my progress as a philosopher of religion and realitologian. I am convinced that the question of truth is central to the study of religion. It would be going too far, however, to claim that the study of religion stands or falls with the question of whether religious language is cognitive or not. The study of religion has many other concerns and would survive even if this question were answered to the detriment of religious cognitivity or even if it were, somehow, banned from the agenda of religious studies.

It is unlikely that the latter would occur, since the question of the *truth* of religions, of their stories and doctrines, will continue to trouble at least some of those intellectuals who turn their attention to the study of religion. For it is through the question of truthfulness, of cognitivity, that the study of religion retains its association with philosophy. Apart from this question, the alliance of the study of religion with sociology, anthropology, folklore, history, and even cognitive science[4] would remain untroubled by the problem of the veridicality of what the religions variously hold as the truth that illumines the mysteries of human life. However, religious people, as opposed to many scholars of religions, are passionately interested in whether what they do and think with respect to the divine is true. This is not for such people merely an intellectual issue, but a concern linked to salvation or liberation, since those who yearn for the release, perfection, or justification promised by religions must believe or hope in the truthfulness of the promise.

Hick is, above all, a champion of this approach to religion *within the study of religion*. He does not want to leave the question of the truth of religions only to the insiders of the various religious traditions. It is for this reason that he argues so forcefully and constantly for a *religious* interpretation of religion as opposed to merely noncognitivist or functionalist interpretations of religion.

Whether these religious views or visions of life are true or even meaningful and how one would go about determining their veridicality if meaningful are, therefore, questions that have exercised John Hick since the beginning of his theological and philosophical career. Long before he came to be identified as an advocate of religious pluralism, Hick had already made a name for himself as a foe of the logical positivists' claim that religious language is not cognitive but rather, at worst, sheer nonsense, or, at best, emotive utterance or poetic expression. Thus, as in the case of religious pluralism, my choice of John Hick as the subject of this book should be obvious. Hick's defense of the cognitivity of religious language long preceded his interest in religious pluralism, though the difficulties associated with defending the cognitivity of religions eventually and logically led him to take up the questions associated with religious pluralism. Both of these concerns will shape the chapters to come, with discussions of religious pluralism logically and chronologically following upon discussions of the cognitivity of religions.

Hick was little concerned in his early writings with issues connected with religious pluralism. In the first decades of his career, he concerned himself rather with the epistemology of religion and the issue of theodicy. His writings in both areas, as well as his later writings on Christology and pluralism, have been widely influential. In this book, I have not concerned myself at all with Hick's innovations with respect to the question of God and evil. I have, however, given considerable effort to attempting to understand Hick's efforts in epistemology, especially with respect to the issue of cognitivity and religious language. I have done so since his later thought, including his evolving views on religious pluralism, directly flows out of these early philosophical efforts.

Hick came of age as a theologian and philosopher of religion during the fifties, when the Anglo-American intellectual world was still standing in the shadow of logical positivism. By the end of the decade, the interests of most philosophers had begun to turn away from this school and its intransigence toward metaphysics and operationally nonverifiable claims to knowledge. However, theologians and philosophers of religions only began to deal with the challenges to religious language posed by this school in the mid-fifties, even though the most virulent attacks had occurred twenty to thirty years before. John Hick first came to prominence in the theological and philosophical communities by throwing himself into the battle for the cognitivity of religious language with his controversial proposal of eschatological verification.

According to this proposal, religious language is not nonsensical, even within the limits allowed by logical positivism and its verification principle. Hick based this proposal on his contention that the claim that God exists—a primary example of religious language being used as a proposition—is meaningful in verificationist terms, since there is an empirical operation that one can perform to verify this claim. Bluntly stated, the operation is death. If, when one dies, one encounters God, then the claim that God exists is retrospectively verified. Hick was convinced that religious language is factual, or cognitive, and therefore meaningful within the limits laid down by the verificationists, not because he *knew* that such an eschatological verification would occur, but simply because it was logically possible. That is, religious language is capable of framing claims that may prove to be either true or false. Thus, religious language cannot be dismissed tout court as nonsensical, as simply poetic and affective, as emotive, or merely as a noncognitive language game.

Inevitably, Hick's proposal was greeted with sharp criticism from all sides. A torrent of articles appeared throughout the sixties attempting to show why eschatological verification is an incoherent proposal. While noting these various criticisms, I develop a critical approach to eschatological verification not taken, as far as I can tell, by any of the others who have subjected this proposal to scrutiny. I take as my starting point the claim that eschatological verification makes use implicitly of the notion of theological analogy, as worked out, for instance, by Thomas Aquinas. I contend that the proposal of eschatological verification is incoherent unless present human existence stands in an analogous relationship with the hypothetical eschatological future that would verify present eschatological speculations. Indeed, apart from such an analogy, one can say nothing at all about the eschaton; one is reduced to equivocation and agnosticism. Hick attempts, with increasing futility, to specify the character of the eschatological future. He appeals first to Jesus, then to God. In each instance, however, the difficulty of specifying how human beings would be able to recognize either entity in a hypothetical future life breaks down. Given the diverse and irreconcilable images of the divine offered not only within Christianity but within the religious traditions of the world, equivocation rather than analogy seems more appropriate when talking about the character and existence of a hypothetical divine reality. Thus, for lack of a clear analogy between present human existence and eschatological existence, Hick, in principle if not in practice, abandons the proposal of eschatological verification.

Hick comes to terms with theological equivocation and the failure of theological analogy to ground eschatological verification by proposing that the diverse ways that religions conceive of the divine be taken not literally but figuratively, or mythologically. At this point, impelled by issues raised by the problem of religious pluralism, Hick moves decisively out of the milieu of verificationism. In his new pluralistic concern to justify the cognitivity of religious languages in general, Hick proposes what he eventually will call the pluralistic hypothesis.

According to this hypothesis, the divine is an unknowable and inexpressible reality that utterly transcends human life and experience. Taking his direction from Kant's First Critique, Hick calls this ineffable reality the Real *an sich*, or the noumenal Real. According to Hick, the noumenal Real is not an object of direct experience, but must, nevertheless, be postulated by religious thinkers, if the interpretation of religious language is not to be characterized as noncognitive by functionalist and nonreligious interpreters of religion. This postulate, in Hick's view, is what distinguishes merely phenomenological from religious interpretations of religion. Thus, the so-called postulate of the noumenal Real, becomes the central pillar in Hick's attempt to develop a "religious" interpretation of religion over against what Hick calls "naturalistic" interpretations of religion, which deny the cognitivity, or referential, dimension of religious language. In this effort of Hick's, the cognitivity of religions and religious pluralism—the themes of this book—come together.

In Hick's view, the noumenal Real is more than just a postulate; it also "affects" human consciousness, thereby instigating the construction of the various personal and impersonal conceptions of the divine that flourish in the many religious traditions of the world. Taking his direction once again from Kant's First Critique, Hick attempts to show how the noumenal Real, supposedly beyond the range of language and experience, comes within range of both through the deployment by the mind of specifically religious categories—God and Absolute—and the schematization, or temporalization, of these categories as the particular divine personalities and impersonal conceptions of the divine that populate the religious life of humanity.

The pluralistic hypothesis, however, is not coherent as it stands. The central flaw of the hypothesis—the claim that the noumenal Real utterly transcends all human experience and knowledge—can never be overcome by any conceptual machinery, even that derived from Kant. If the Real *an sich* is, as Hick contends, beyond speech, knowledge, and experience, then one has no choice but to remain silent about it. However, if this is the way it is with the noumenal Real, then it shows itself to be otiose, doing no real work in Hick's pluralistic hypothesis.[5]

Given this theoretical failure, Hick pushes the hypothesis in a practical direction, making the cognitivity of religions to depend not on their relationship to the ineffable Real *an sich* but rather on their conformity to what Hick calls *the soteriological principle*, or the claim that all post-axial religions are more or less true insofar as each fosters the transformation whereby an individual becomes less centered upon the self and more centered upon the Real. However, this move results in a reductionism that drains the religious traditions of their doctrinal and narrative richness, since what is relevant to this soteriological approach is not the polysemic contents of doctrines and stories but whether they induce one to be a better person. This approach is offensive to the insiders of various traditions, since the stories and doctrines of the various traditions have meaning for these believers quite apart from their strictly practical consequences.

Because of these and other failings, I reject Hick's quasi-Kantian pluralistic hypothesis. However, I respect his efforts in this area, even if I disagree with much of what he has done. That he has tried to mitigate religious absolutism and exclusivism as well as uphold the cognitivity of religions is more significant than the circumstance that his specific proposals toward these ends have been unworkable. Thus, in keeping with the spirit of Hick's efforts in this area, I will propose a new version of the pluralistic hypothesis, one that might have come from Hick's own pen had he not, inexplicably, strayed into quasi Kantianism but, rather, further developed notions that are central to his thought from his earliest writings. These notions have been characterized by Hick as *the cognitive ambiguity of the universe, human cognitive freedom, faith as interpretation,* and *the rationality of trusting one's own experience.* I think that if Hick had developed these ideas rather than turning to Kant's First Critique he would have developed a far more convincing analysis of religious pluralism and religious cognitivity than the one that he proposes in his recent writings.

Notes

[1] Gavin D'Costa provides a summary biography of Hick, which makes use of the same sources to which I refer, in *John Hick's Theology of Religions: A Critical Evaluation* (Lanham, MD: University Press of America, 1987), 5–16.

[2] Paul Knitter writes: "If Vatican II is a watershed in Christian attitudes toward other religions, Karl Rahner is its chief engineer. His 1961 study on Christianity and non-Christian religions broke new ground; so did his earlier and more foundational investigations into the relation between nature and grace and between universal and special salvation history. With these bold explorations into unfamiliar theological territory, Rahner not only prepared the way for Vatican II but indirectly contributed to much of its substance. Subsequently, he attempted to show how the council opened doors to a genuinely new stage in the history of the church—an opening, he suggests, of which many of the conciliar fathers were not fully aware" (*No Other Name? A Critical Survey of Christian Attitudes Toward the World Religions* [Maryknoll, NY: Orbis Books, 1985], 125).

[3] The Barthian notion of the Christian gospel as a *crisis* or judgment of God upon

other religions was developed by Hendrik Kraemer, a Dutch missionary to Java and historian of religions, whose neo-Reformation theology of religions dominated mainstream Protestant thought about other religions from the 1938 meeting of International Missions Council at Tambaram (near Madras) until Hick's call for a Copernican revolution in theology in 1972. Summarizing Kraemer's view, Wesley Ariarajah, writes: "Kraemer joined with Karl Barth in making a sharp distinction between revelation and religion, and supported the view that all religions including empirical Christianity were under the judgment of God's revelation in Christ. The gospel, therefore, was the crisis of all religions, which were human achievements curtailed by man's sinful rebellion against God's holy will. The gospel was not in continuity but in discontinuity with man's religious life, for it called him from disbelief to an act of faith in what God had done in Christ" (*Hindus and Christians: A Century of Protestant Ecumenical Thought* [Grand Rapids, MI: William B. Eerdmans Publishing Company, 1991], 66). See Hendrik Kraemer, *The Christian Message in a Non-Christian World*, 2nd ed. (New York: International Missionary Council, 1946), 123–30 for a fuller exposition of this position. See also paragraph 17 of Karl Barth's *Church Dogmatics* for the theological basis of Kraemer's view of religions.

[4] For a recent attempt to provide a scientific *and* religious account of meditative experience from the standpoint of cognitive science, see Charles D. Laughlin, John McManus, and Eugene G. d'Aquili, *Brain, Symbol, and Experience: Toward a Neurophenomenology of Human Consciousness* (Boston: Shambhala, 1990). A record of a 1991 dialogue between representatives of Tibetan Buddhist psychology and meditation and Western cognitive sciences has been published as *Mind-Science: An East-West Dialogue,* edited by Daniel Goleman and Robert A. F. Thurman (Boston: Wisdom Publications, 1991).

[5] Stephen Grover, "Unmatching Mysteries," review of *An Interpretation of Religion: Human Responses to the Transcendent*, by John Hick, *Times Literary Supplement*, 22–28 Dec. 1989.

2

Eschatological Verification

The belief that religions have a cognitive dimension, that is, that they are realistic in intention because they refer to realities external to the language and practices of religious communities, runs through all of John Hick's writings. Hick has tried to defend this realistic, or cognitivist, interpretation of religion in two major ways: one is his proposal of eschatological verification; the other is the pluralistic hypothesis. Both of these strategies have had significant impact upon the interpretation of religions and religious language in the fields of theology and philosophy of religion.

Prior to developing the pluralistic hypothesis,[1] Hick's basic strategy for defending the realist intention of religions was his proposal of eschatological verification, a project that, as we will see, is increasingly beset with the difficulty of satisfactorily specifying the eschatological *verificandum*.[2] This difficulty is exacerbated by Hick's increasingly receptive encounter with religious traditions other than Christianity and their diverse eschatological scenarios. The proposal of eschatological verification in the end proves incapable of meeting the challenge posed for defining the eschatological *verificandum* by this eschatological diversity. Yet, despite the evident failure of his eschatological proposal, Hick has never repudiated it; paradoxically, he continues to apply it in his latest writings. Thus, in *An Interpretation of Religion* (1989), he extends it to the eschatologies of Hinduism and Buddhism, with unacceptable results.

Hick was prompted by the challenge of the verification principle to propose eschatological verification as a way of demonstrating that the claim that God exists is not meaningless, as was
held by leading logical positivists. In Hick's view the possibility of
experiential confirmation of God's existence is "built into the
Christian concept of God" (*EG*, 260). The proposal of eschatological verification is designed by Hick to bring out this aspect of
the concept of God.

That which constitutes verification of the claim that God exists cannot be mere survival of death, for even Moritz Schlick—
certainly no theist—accepted that one could by dying be in a position to verify that life continues beyond the demise of one's body.
Hick, however, wants more from eschatological verification than
this. He argues that the claim that God exists would be verified
only if a survivor encounters God in the afterdeath state (should
there be such a state).[3] This raises the central issue for eschatological verification when it is conceived not merely as a way of verifying continued existence after physical death but also of verifying
the existence of God: How will God be recognized *as God* in the
hypothetical afterstate by those who survive death?

This question, whether explicitly or implicitly stated, motivates Hick's thirty-year long conceptual wriggling over the nature
of the *verificandum*. Is God to be recognized after death as the
verificandum directly, through the mediation of Jesus Christ,
through a complex encounter with God in a series of postmortem
existences, or through the recognition of the illusoriness of sepa-
rate selves, as in Hindu and Buddhist philosophy? Except for the
last possibility, the theological principle of analogy is implicated
in all of these *verificandum*-candidates. This suggests that what
enables those who survive death to verify the claim that God exists is an encounter, whether simple or complex, direct or indirect,
with a reality or entity that eminently, or perfectly, instantiates

essential human attributes. It is this similarity, or analogy, between the human and the divine reality that, in principle, makes recognition of God by survivors, and thus verification that God exists, possible. Although not apparent at first glance, eschatological verification depends upon the theological principle of analogy, as classically enunciated, for instance, by Thomas Aquinas. This dependency increasingly becomes clear as Hick struggles to conceive the nature of the *verificandum*.

That this appeal to analogy is ultimately futile becomes evident when Hick tries to extend eschatological verification to certain Hindu and Buddhist eschatologies that bear no resemblance to ordinary human experience. Analogy fails to find purchase when projected upon Brahman and *nirvāṇa*, the eschatological futures proposed by certain Hindu religious philosophies and by Buddhist philosophy, respectively. This outcome supports Hick's increasing recognition of the failure of analogy to illumine the eschatological future proposed in the version of Christianity that he articulates.

Consequently, Hick eventually in principle, though not in practice, gives up both the principle of analogy and the proposal of eschatological verification. He begins to move toward the transcendental agnosticism and appeal to myth characteristic of the pluralistic hypothesis, which in principle involves the rejection of analogical predication in favor of equivocal predication. The latter form of predication implies no relationship between essential human attributes and the reality encountered in the eschaton. With the breaking of the bond of analogy, however, eschatological verification loses its force. For the Real *an sich*, which in Hick's definition is unknowable and inexpressible, can no longer be understood as that which will verify the various eschatologies proposed by various religions. In the face of the transcendent mystery of the

Real *an sich*, all theological language must be understood as mythological in character.

Eschatological Verification

Eschatological verification[4] was criticized soon after Hick proposed it in 1960 as a "desperate move."[5] Hick responded that "'eschatological verification' is not a desperate *ad hoc* device invented to meet a skeptical challenge but draws out that aspect of the traditional theistic system of belief which establishes that system as a complex factual assertion" (*PRP, 123*).

This aspect of traditional theism (by which term Hick means Christian theism and its picture of the universe) entails

> certain distinctive expectations concerning the future [which] is a very different picture from any that can be accepted by one who does not believe that the God of the New Testament exists. Further, these differences are such as to show themselves in human experience. The possibility of experiential confirmation [verification] is thus built into the concept of God; and the notion of eschatological verification seeks to relate this fact to the problem of theological meaning (*EG, 260*).

Hick denies that his proposal is merely an expedient apologetic device motivated solely by the challenge of verificationism. Rather, it is a way of defining the cognitive aspect of theism so as directly to respond to the challenge of verificationism. The claim that religions have a cognitive dimension is not a new claim about religions, made only after the verificationist assault on religious knowledge. On the contrary, religious believers in general have always, consciously or unconsciously, believed and acted as if the view of the world generated by their religious beliefs is true to the nature of reality.[6] Traditionally, religion and knowledge were never separated; indeed, religion traditionally offered the highest and most secure path of knowledge.[7] That ancient certainty has eroded for many modern Westerners, yet for most modern believers the connection between religious beliefs and knowledge—their cognitivity—remains, even when it functions as no more than an undefended or unarticulated intuition.

The concept of cognitivity that informs Hick's development of the proposal of eschatological verification is strictly verificationist. In this phase of Hick's thought he used "cognitive" as a synonym for *factually meaningful*, which was how the word was used by logical positivists.[8] In contrast to emotivist or pragmatic uses of a sentence, a cognitive, or factually meaningful, sentence expresses either an analytic statement or an empirically verifiable statement, which is potentially capable of being shown to be either true or false or to some degree probable on the basis of empirical observations.[9] On the basis of such a view of cognitivity, Hick formulated a verification principle that would be broad enough to include religious claims:

> A genuine assertion, as a putative statement of fact, must lay itself open to correction and refutation. It must commit itself to something being there which might conceivably turn out not to be there, or to something happening which might not happen, or happening in this way when it might instead happen in that way. The maxim applies, "nothing venture, nothing gain"; in order to achieve a meaningful assertion we must be willing to run the risk of error. In order to say something which may possibly be true we must say something which may possibly be false. The underlying principle may be stated as follows: if a proposition p is to constitute a (true or false) assertion, the state of the universe which satisfies p must differ, other than in the fact of including this assertion, from any state of the universe that satisfies *not-p* (FK1, 147).[10]

A proposition that fulfills this criterion is a cognitive, or factually meaningful, statement, i.e., one that is subject to verification. In clarifying this principle, Hick is careful to define a statement as factual "in terms of the making of an actual or possible difference within human experience"(FP, 249).[11] In its simplest terms, then, Hick's verification principle amounts to the claim that to be considered cognitive an utterance must refer to some *experientially pos-*

sible state of the world. On the basis of this liberal (or Feiglian) version of the verification principle, it may be claimed that cognitive (or factually meaningful) statements are not only those that have been shown to be true or false, but also those that are *conceivably* true or false but whose truth-value is as yet undetermined. In light of this version of the verification principle, a posteriori theological claims are just as much subject to verification as any other kind of statement about any conceivable state of affairs. From Hick's standpoint, therefore, the main difference between a cognitivist theologian and an atheistic or antireligious scientific empiricist or naturalist is not a different standard for existence-claims but rather a different view of what is experientially *possible*.[12]

Having formulated his own version of the verification principle, Hick is now in position to address the question of whether theism is an experimental issue, that is, whether the claim that God exists is confirmable, or experienceable, in principle (*FK1*, 145). Applying his liberal version of the verification principle to theology, Hick imagines that the verificationist would challenge the theist with questions such as:

> How do you suppose the present state of the universe to differ from the state in which it would be if there were no God? What do you *deny* by your assertion that there is a God? What does the theistic assertion allege to exist or to happen or to happen thus, which might conceivably fail to exist or occur or which might occur otherwise? At what point, in short, does it lay itself open to confirmation or refutation? (*FK1*, 147)

Hick's answer to these questions takes the form of the proposal of eschatological verification, which will be discussed later in this section. Hick notes that questions of this sort, which were implicit in the logical positivists' critique of theology, were not treated "with any depth" by theologians until the publication in 1944 of "Gods," a classical essay by the philosopher John Wisdom on the logical analysis of theological language (*FK1*, 145). According to Hick, "Gods" and the parable of the gardener contained in it inspired other logical analysts of theology to take up the question of whether theism—centrally involving the question of whether God exists—is an experimental issue (which is the central problem with theistic language from the verificationist standpoint) (*FK1*, 145).[13]

In "Gods," Wisdom addresses this question by introducing the familiar gardener parable in which two travelers return to their long neglected but still partially vigorous garden and argue over whether a gardener has been tending it. When the neighbors say that they haven't seen anyone working in the garden, one of the travelers opines that perhaps the gardener came while the neighbors slept. The other traveler replies that someone would have heard the gardener and, besides, the gardener would have kept the weeds down. There can be no agreement between the two travelers, because where one sees beauty and design in the overgrown garden the other sees evidence of a lack of care and even of a malicious hand. Thus, they come to a standstill: one traveler believes that a gardener still comes, while the other sees no reason to accept this hypothesis. At this point in the parable, Wisdom concludes that the gardener hypothesis is not experimental; the difference between the two travelers is not a matter of different evidence, for they both agree about the present overgrown and disordered condition of the garden, but rather a matter of how they *feel* toward the garden.[14]

The gardener parable is more familiar in the version presented by Antony Flew in his short and highly influential essay "Theology and Falsification."[15] There are several differences between Flew's and Wisdom's version of the parable, the most important being that in Flew's version two explorers happen upon a *clearing* in the forest where both weeds and flowers are growing. This change is an improvement, for it reflects the actual human situation: both theists and atheists face the world and discover signs of both apparent care and inattention in it. In Wisdom's version, there seems to be a slight bias toward a theistic view, or perhaps a deistic view, since the two travelers return to *their long neglected garden.* Flew drops this aspect of Wisdom's parable, thus making the contest between the theist and the nontheist more equal.[16] He agrees with Wisdom that differentiating between the view that a gardener comes (theism) and the view that no gardener comes (atheism) cannot be an experimental issue, since the evidence adduced by the theist and the atheist is the same. Since no experiment can be devised to decide between the two hypotheses, they are testably equivalent.[17] However, Flew draws out the point of the parable with more force than does Wisdom when he asks the theist: "What would have to occur or to have occurred to constitute for you a disproof of the love of, or of the existence of, God."[18]

This provocative question instigated much of the subsequent controversy between philosophical theists and verificationists and can be seen as motivating much of Hick's thinking on this topic, which has continued from the first edition of *Faith and Knowledge* through his most recent statements about eschatological verification.[19]

Hick agrees that the ambiguity of the evidence available to both theist and atheist suggests that theism may not be an experimental issue (*FK1*, 145). A consistent atheistic interpretation, able to account not only for the general facts of nature but also for all the special phenomena of religion, cannot experimentally be shown in any crucial instance to be indisputably more or less comprehensive than a theistic interpretation of the same phenomena. Thus, in Hick's view, there is no way to decide conclusively between theistic and atheistic interpretations of the same evidence (*FK1*, 145; *EG*, 260; *IR*, 12).[20]

Although agreeing with this conclusion, Hick was not ready to abandon the cognitivity of religious claims. He rose to the challenge of the gardener parable not by attempting a defense of the cognitivity of theistic language *on the basis of present evidence* (*FK1*, 147-48), but by substituting another parable. In Hick's parable, one of two travelers on an unfamiliar road is convinced that the road leads to a Celestial City, while the other believes that it leads nowhere. They both meet with times of refreshment and delight, hardship and danger. One sees these as the trials and blessings of a pilgrimage designed to make him a good citizen of the kingdom to which he is journeying, while the other sees the journey as an unavoidable and aimless ramble that must simply be endured (*EG*, 260; *FK1*, 150).

Hick's parable, which is patterned after the gardener parable, concedes the *present* but not the *future* equivalence of evidence for the two hypotheses.[21] Since each of these perspectives can account consistently for all the data that they *presently* share in common, there is no way on the basis of *present* evidence to decide between the views. In Hick's view, the present evidence allows either conclusion—namely, that human beings are intelligent animals, produced by evolution and destined to extinction when the environment becomes inhospitable for them, or that human beings partake of a spiritual reality that is not negated by the death of the body (*FK1*, 150). Only *retrospectively*, through an afterdeath encounter with God as mediated by Jesus Christ that assures the survivor of the fulfillment of God's purposes for his or her life, could the theistic assertion be proven (*EG*, 269).[22] The possibility that this may occur in a hypothetical future life is, in Hick's view, the "experiential crux" (*FK1*, 150) between theism and atheism that negates the claim that they are testably equivalent hypotheses.

This view, which secures the meaningfulness of the claim that God exists because of its potential for *future* confirmation, is the core of the proposal of eschatological verification.[23]

Eschatological Verification and the Theological Principle of Analogy

Differing from the numerous interpretations of Hick's proposal of eschatological verification that have been suggested over the past three decades,[24] I will now propose a new and more fundamental interpretation by examining the theological principle of analogy upon which it relies. In my opinion, the validity of eschatological verification stands or falls upon the possibility of discovering enduring analogies between present human experience and the ultimate eschatological future of humankind, whether it be conceived as God, Christ, the Real, Brahman, or any other of the virtually infinite conceptions of the divine that the human imagination has generated over the millennia. One must consider whether eschatological hope, which informs the consciousness of most religious people, is a legitimate response to the mysteries of destiny and death with which our individual and collective lives are inescapably inscribed. This question will be the driving force behind the following interpretation of eschatological verification. It is my contention that apart from an analogical relationship between present human existence and the consummation promised in the various eschatologies, eschatological speculation is groundless.

The theological use of the principle of analogy, which can be traced back to Plato[25] and Aristotle,[26] was given its classical and still unsurpassed definition by Thomas Aquinas:

> Some words are used neither univocally nor purely equivocally of creatures, but analogically, for we cannot speak of God at all except in the language we use of creatures, and so whatever is said both of God and

creatures is said in virtue of the order that creatures have to God as to their source and cause in which all perfections of things pre-exist transcendently [i.e., superexcellently, or eminently]. This way of using words lies somewhere between pure equivocation and simple univocity [*Et iste modus communitatis medius est inter puram aequivocationem et simplicem univocationem*], for the word is neither used in the same sense, as with univocal usage, nor in totally different senses, as with equivocation.[27]

Herbert McCabe suggests a contemporary definition of analogy as a relation that is "common to diverse objects by a likeness that is more than verbal (*equivocal*) yet does not amount to specific or generic sameness (*univocal*)."[28] Outside of Thomistic circles the validity of theological analogy has been severely criticized and dismissed as invalid.[29] Despite the devastating criticisms of analogy, it remains a method thought by some contemporary thinkers still to possess great usefulness, thinkers who would find the critics of analogy to be unduly influenced by empiricism and Kant. Thus, David Burrell, a contemporary interpreter of Thomas Aquinas, writes that the aim of analogical reasoning is "to secure the distinction of God from the world, and to do so in such a way as to display how such a One, who must be unknowable, may also be known. The exercise is clearly a philosophical one, however theological be its goal."[30]

Underlying the analogical mode of reasoning is the notion that creatures proceed from a first uncaused cause, which they strive to replicate, despite their finitude. Thomas writes that "these names [*good, wise*, and the like] signify the divine substance, and are predicated substantially of God, although they fall short of a full representation of Him."[31] Herbert McCabe glosses this claim:

[Thomas] attaches great importance to the idea that such words [*good, wise*, etc.] apply "primarily" to God. The point of this seems to be that when you "try to mean" God's goodness by using the word "good" of him, you are not straying outside its normal meaning but trying to enter more deeply into it.[32]

Thus, theological language, according to Thomas and his followers, is most rightly construed as theomorphic, not anthropomorphic, for God is the superexcellent yet simple being from whom all perfections flow.[33] This is not to deny the *human* origin of such terms as *good* and *wise*, but rather to assert that whatever meaning they have in human experience is derived ultimately from the abundance and excellence of the divine reality. As Thomas writes:

> For the words, *God is good*, or *wise*, signify not only that He is the cause of wisdom or goodness, but that these exist in Him in a more excellent way. Hence as regards what the name signifies, these names are applied primarily to God rather than to creatures because these perfections flow from God to creatures; but as regards the imposition of names, they are primarily applied by us to creatures which we know first.[34]

Thus, to say that God is wise is to say that God is the "very source and norm of [that] wisdom"[35] of which human wisdom is a lesser reflection. The same may be said for the other perfections of God that, according to analogical reasoning, human beings are said to possess, such as goodness, life, and justice.

Traditionally, the theological use of analogy is the attempt to work out a conception of God by drawing analogies between created realities and the mystery of God and the eternal life of God, which orthodox Christian doctrine holds will be shared in by the blessed. I want to extend this use by applying it to eschatology. Specifically, I want to make explicit what is implicit in Hick's proposal of eschatological verification: analogy underlies the ability of the survivor to recognize God (or Jesus Christ, Brahman, and so forth) in the afterlife and thus verify the claim that God exists. This recognition occurs when the survivor understands herself to be in the presence of one who exemplifies superexcellently valued human attributes, such as love, goodness, wisdom, justice, and so forth. This principle, it seems to me, underlies the eschatological speculations of all human beings, including that of Hick.[36]

Applying this definition of theological analogy to Hick's proposal of eschatological verification, I will ask whether central attributes of human beings (such as personal identity, conscience, thinking, emotion, will, desire, memory, gregariousness, and religiousness) have analogous attributes in that entity, however it may be characterized, believed by eschatologists to be encountered in the eschaton. (I do not intend to deal with these attributes individually, but with the general question of whether analogy can reasonably support the eschatological hope and speculations that seem nearly universal among human beings.) The outcome of this inquiry pertains to the validity of eschatological verification, since if there is no likeness between present human experience and the superexcellent entity hypothetically encountered in the afterlife, it is impossible that any proposition about the eschaton can be meaningful.

Hick's view of the usefulness of analogy (which he sometimes refers to by the term "continuities"[DEL, 22])[37] for justifying eschatological verification has changed considerably over the decades. His view of analogy has always been ambivalent, though he took an affirmative stance toward analogy in *Christianity at the Centre* (1970):

> The perfecting of our own human nature ... must be a part of the ultimate confirming situation. We cannot now concretely visualize the nature of this perfection even though we glimpse aspects of it in all that is best in the human spirit. But the fact that we cannot now describe it does not necessarily mean that the situation itself would not be identifiable by one who participates in it. A little child is unable to conceive what it will be like to be grown up; but as he grows his understanding of adulthood also grows so that he has no difficulty in recognizing that state when he has reached it. And the fulfillment of God's purpose for mankind may be as remote from our present human condition as is adult maturity from the mind of a baby. But any development towards it will involve a growing ap-

preciation of the nature of that fulfillment so that the problem of recognition will disappear in the process (CC, 106).

This position, by relating present human existence to the ultimate eschatological confirming situation—an encounter with a superexcellent reality—implicitly involves the use of analogy because it asserts that there is an essential link between the dimensions of present human experience and the reality hypothetically encountered in the eschaton. It is this essential link, elaborated in the analogies stated above, that suggest that our present imperfect human existence, shot through as it is with ineffable but irrepressible yearnings for perfection, will find its fulfillment in an eschatological encounter with a being that is commensurate, though eminently, or superexcellently, with our present existence.

Pushing the Limits of Analogy

However, Hick has been doubtful about the usefulness of analogy, as in the following quote, also from *Christianity at the Centre:*

> The special problem confronting the notion of eschatological verification is this: how are we to postulate sufficient correlation [analogy] between the Christian's present expectations and a future situation of unambiguous divine rule, in view of the admitted vagueness of these expectations? How could a heavenly world be recognized as confirming Christian faith? (CC, 105)

This doubt about analogy is radicalized in Hick's later writings, as evidenced in the following quote from *Death and Eternal Life* (1976):

> Certain basic continuities [analogies] must hold if we are to speak of individual identity and life. . . . But there are reasons . . . to suppose that no mode of existence *analogous* to our present life could continue forever, through unlimited time. And when we try to think beyond this to an eternal, transtemporal destiny, we are trying to conceive of something be-

yond the reach even of our most ambitious imagining (*DEL*, 22 emphasis mine).

Hick questions analogy even more drastically in *An Interpretation of Religion* (1989), where he writes that the eschaton may "from our present point of view consist in such a completely altered state of consciousness as to be beyond the scope of our present imagining" (*IR*, 179). He further claims that the eschaton is "not only unimaginable but also conceptually ungraspable by us"(*IR*, 355). However, if this should be the case, then no statement about the eschaton framed in any human language (given that languages are constructed in relation to the dimensions of *present* human life) could be said to be factually meaningful, since none of them is potentially verifiable. On this view, analogy would be of no help in supporting the factuality of theological language.[38]

If this were all that there were to Hick's proposal it would dissolve in contradiction at this point. For on the one hand he wants to devise a cognitively valid test for theism, to be applied eschatologically, while on the other he seems to deny that any test can apply to that which utterly transcends human experience. To avoid contradiction, Hick must assert one of the following propositions: either some aspects of human experience are analogous to the superexcellent reality hypothetically encountered in the eschaton or human experience and the eschaton are radically different from each other. The former assertion would preserve the link essential to eschatological verification, while the latter assertion would undermine analogy and, therefore, eschatological verification, thereby opening the door to what Gavin D'Costa calls "transcendent agnosticism."[39]

At first this dilemma little troubled Hick, as evidenced by his originally conceiving the *verificandum* in literalistic, orthodox terms. In the earliest versions of eschatological verification, Hick's *verificandum* consisted in an eschatological awareness that God's purposes for one's life had been fulfilled in an experience of communion with Jesus Christ, who is encountered as reigning over the Kingdom of his Father. As Hick writes:

> It is God's union with man in Christ that makes possible man's recognition [in the eschaton] of the fulfillment of God's purpose for man as being indeed the fulfillment of *God's* purpose for him. The presence of Christ in [God's] Kingdom marks this as being beyond doubt the Kingdom of the God and the Father of the Lord Jesus Christ (*EG*, 271–72).

This version of eschatological verification now seems surprisingly naive,[40] as Hick himself has gradually come to see.[41] In his first book, *Faith and Knowledge* (first edition, 1957), Hick expressed an equally naive and optimistic view of the *verificandum* when he claimed that in the eschatological Kingdom "the human mind will see all things as God sees them, apprehending at last their full significance and nature" (*FK1*, 160). However, this view fails to come to terms with the problem of how finite beings will be able to recognize a being of infinite attributes.[42] If God, being infinite, is so radically different and unanticapatable that in order to encounter God human beings must no longer be finite but rather infinite (as represented by the Hindu metaphor of the river merging with the ocean),[43] then the validity of eschatological verification is nullified. This is because earthly and resurrection bodies are *as bodies* finite individuals existing within communities of other finite individuals and thus cannot be mediums of infinite knowledge. Infinite knowledge transcends the limits of human existence, whether that existence be carbon-based, silicon-based, or spirit-based.[44] Consequently, if only an infinite knower can verify that God exists, and no human being—not even a resurrected human being—is an infinite knower, then no human knower can ever verify that God exists.[45] Thus, no finite test—such as eschatological verification—can be the criterion of an infinite reality (*PRP*, 120-21), since the validity of eschatological verification depends upon the possibility of articulating in terms of finite language and experience some set of propositions as possible candidates for verification in the eschaton. If this is not a possibility, then no *literal* meaning can be applied to the claim that human beings will know all things as God knows them. This outcome further undermines the legitimacy of theological analogy, which depends for its usefulness upon tracing created attributes, such as knowledge, justice, wisdom, love, and personhood, back to their divine source—a procedure that, if the foregoing conclusions are warranted, is found wanting.

Hick tried to circumvent these unwanted results in his well-known article "Theology and Verification" (1960) through recourse to a neo-orthodox conception of Jesus Christ, as summarized in a line that he quoted from Karl Barth: "Jesus Christ is the knowability of God" (*EG*, 270–71).[46] Hick interpreted this phrase to mean that although no finite being *in via* or *in patria*[47] can actually observe the presence of an infinite God, finite beings can become persuaded of the existence of God *in patria* through an encounter with Jesus Christ, who reigns in God's Kingdom with the full authority of God the Father (*EG*, 272). Thus, the mediating of finite human experience and the infinite God by the God-Man Jesus Christ justifies asserting the validity of the principle of analogy and, along with it, the proposal of eschatological verification.

However, positing Jesus as *verificandum* raises the issue of how one will identify Jesus in the eschaton. Certainty that the sublime personage encountered eschatologically *is* Jesus will be no more available to a finite knower than certainty that an infinite God exists. The difficulty that Hick rejects with respect to God also affects his reliance upon Jesus, for he assumes that Jesus *will* be easily recognizable. Yet what physical feature would persuade us that it is Jesus whom we are meeting? Will he wear a robe? A beard? Long hair? Will he be the Jesus of the preaching missions?

Of the Passion? Of the Resurrection appearances? Of Paul's preaching? Or the white-haired Judge bearing a rod of iron while seated upon the Great White Throne of Judgment, as described in Revelation? Will he appear like a lamb that was slain? What color and race will he be? Will we first have to put our hands in his scars before we could say that this lordly being whom we were meeting is Jesus? Will his cross be nearby, and Mary, his mother? Will the twelve apostles or the succession of the popes be present to lend their authority to our recognition that this noble being whom we are encountering is indeed Jesus Christ?[48] Paul was no doubt aware of this problem when he quoted the Apocalypse of Elijah: "As it is written: 'No eye has seen, no ear has heard, no mind has conceived what God has prepared for those who love him.'"[49]

If this passage, which negates eschatological analogy, is true, then Christians will not have any of the figural, biographical, or historical details of Christian doctrine or scriptures to help them eschatologically to verify that either the God of Jesus Christ or Jesus Christ himself exists. Thus, Hick's reliance upon Jesus still involves a crude, simplistic verificandum.

Hick eventually surrendered the belief that encounter with Jesus eschatologically would indirectly verify that God exists, a move that was controversial for his fellow Christians.[50] Hick decided instead that the verification of the claim that God exists is complex and not to be satisfied by a simple observation that God (or, for that matter, Jesus) is present in the afterdeath state (*PRP*, 116).[51] In a *complex* verification, the claim that God exists is *progressively* verified as individuals transit through a series of "various intermediate [postmortem] environments" toward perfection in the presence of an infinite and invisible God. One can't just go "to heaven" and observe God there,[52] since what is to be verified eschatologically is no longer the "isolable and bounded fact" proposed by the statement "God exists," but rather the more complex assertion that "the theistic account of the character of the universe, and of what is taking place in its history, is true" (*PRP*, 115–16).

Despite this change from a simple to a complex *verificandum*, Hick's basic argument remained the same: the possibility that a religious belief will be confirmed eschatologically justifies its presently being taken as cognitive, or factually meaningful. The eschatological persistence of personhood through an enlightening series of postmortem experiences, an ascent through successive stages of being in which the reality of God or Jesus Christ is incrementally realized would constitute a progressive verification of the claims of theism and a vindication of the validity of the principle of analogy.[53]

Although Hick attempted in this way to retain his explicit confidence in eschatological verification and his implicit reliance on the principle of analogy, his conception of the hypothetical super-excellent reality with which theological claims and analogies are concerned underwent a notable revision as a result of his increasing openness to religious traditions other than Christianity.[54] This openness, in concert with his growing recognition that the *verificandum* must be complex, motivated him to extend the application of eschatological verification beyond the verification of simple or complex propositions of Christian theology to the plural and divergent truth claims of the different religions of the world (*PRP*, 121, 124-25; *IR*, 175-88). He now argued that such diverse teachings as the Christian notion of the Kingdom of God, the Hindu doctrine of *mokṣa*—the experience of the sublation of all individual souls (*jīvas*) in a single consciousness, or Brahman (*IR*, 180-82), and Buddhist claims that suffering beings may find freedom by experiencing reality (variously termed *nirvāṇa, śūnyatā, dharmakāya, dharmadhātu*) derive their factuality, or cognitivity, from the *possibility* that any of them may be verified eschatologically (*IR*, 183-87).

This modification of eschatological verification is a dubious development, for the application of a test designed originally for the simple question of whether one encounters God or Jesus Christ when one dies produces a jarring dissonance when applied to doctrines like the celebrated Upaniṣadic dictum "All is Brahman."[55] Hick admits to an increasing elusiveness in conceiving how such a statement may be eschatologically verified (*IR*, 183),[56] for it is far more difficult to form a conception of the content of Brahman or *nirvāṇa* than it is to form a conception of Jesus or a personal God. This is because Jesus and the God of Jesus, being conceived as eschatological *persons*, are closer to present human experience than the *transpersonal*, nondual Brahman, which is often conceptualized as a universal unity in which all distinctions are sublated. Because transpersonal eschatologies are so remote from ordinary *human* experience, it is difficult to imagine how Brahman or *nirvāṇa* could be verified eschatologically. For if the ultimate telos of the individual self is a return to the infinite (Brahman in Advaita Vedānta[57] or *nirvāṇa* in Buddhism), then it may well be that there is no presently or retrospectively conceivable analogy between current human experience and that eminent reality which, hypothetically, is encountered in the eschaton. For the reversion of the individual to the infinite would negate the finitude and modes of awareness of finite beings and thus of the basis of analogy and eschatological verification.

Hick is not without an answer to this serious charge against the validity of eschatological verification—though it is a desperate one. He admits that although "the conditions which have to be met in order to experience this end-state [the sublation of the finite self by Brahman] are extremely arduous [they do] not affect the logical relationship of prediction and fulfillment" between present experience and the eschatological endstate (*IR*, 181). He offers the following *ad hoc* explanation of how such a verification may occur in the case of Advaita Vedānta:

> Let us suppose that when individuals reach a certain level of spiritual development (*mokṣa*) they fuse mentally with all others who have attained the same level; and that eventually *all* fuse in this way. There then exists a universal consciousness which is the *successor* of each of the individual streams of consciousness. Advaita Vedānta adds that the separate consciousnesses were merely fleeting swirls of cloudy delusion obscuring the perfect clarity of the universal consciousness, Brahman. If, then, in the eschaton all consciousnesses have united into a single consciousness, and if this was predicted in a theory propounded by some of the individual consciousnesses before they united, it would seem that the unitary consciousness may be said to have verified that theory in its own experience. The eternal Self will know (and indeed now knows) that It is the one ultimate Reality underlying the illusorily finite egos. And if the advaitic doctrine is true this would seem to be the kind of experiential verification that is appropriate to its being true (*IR*, 182-83).

This implausible scenario is subject to the criticism that the verifier in this case is no longer *and indeed never was*[58] a particular finite individual, as in the Christian personalistic eschatology. Furthermore, it goes against the spirit of Advaita Vedānta to attribute a quasi-personalistic mentality—that of a verifying observer—to *nirguṇa* Brahman, which is a transpersonal reality so utterly different from ordinary human experience that only equivocal and never analogous language can be used when speaking of it.[59]

The same consequence results from an examination not only of Hindu but also of Christian eschatological speculation, for one may ask what test can there be for the reality of God, classically conceived, if we can know God as God knows Godself only at the moment of God's absolute self-revelation *in patria*, a revelation that would dissolve or render inoperative the barrier between finite and infinite existence and knowledge?[60]

From these two examples it is clear that if the eminent reality hypothetically encountered in the postmortem state is disanalogous to present human experience, then it is futile to look to that reality for a verification of propositions conceived within the limits of finite comprehension. This outcome would undermine eschatological verification, since propositions stated within the confines of finite human languages would neither be verifed by an infinite, transpersonal eschatological reality nor guarantee the factualness of any particular eschatological doctrine of any religious tradition.[61] Furthermore, the speculative and anticipatory making of analogies by the human spirit of its ultimate terminus in the various religious traditions would be frustrated without hope of recompense if the final endstate were disanalogous to present human experience. Thus, eschatological verification appears to be a futile proposal.

Eschatologies and Pareschatologies

Before working out the position to which he now adheres, Hick addressed the above criticism in *Death and Eternal Life* (1976) by distinguishing between *eschatologies*, or "'pictures' of the ultimate state (which may well transcend individual existence as we now know it)" and *pareschatologies*, or "'pictures' of what happens between death and the ultimate state"(*DEL*, 12, 22). He explains this distinction in the following way:

> If there is life after death there may be a better possibility of picturing its more proximate than its more ultimate phases. It will therefore be useful to distinguish between pareschatologies and eschatologies. Whereas eschatology is the doctrine of the *eschata* or last things, and thus of the ultimate state of man, pareschatology is, by analogy, the doctrine of the *para-eschata*, or next-to-last things, and thus of the human future between the present life and man's ultimate state. And it may well be possible to speculate more profitably about pareschatology than about eschatology. For if there is continued existence after bodily death it is possible that its more immediate phases may bear *sufficient analogy* to our present state for some of our speculations about it not to be wholly misleading. . . . But there are reasons . . . to suppose that no mode of existence analogous to

our present life could continue for ever, through unlimited time. And when we try to think beyond this to an eternal, transtemporal destiny we are trying to conceive of something beyond the reach even of our most ambitious imaginings (*DEL*, 22, emphasis mine).

Hick here distinguishes between traditional eschatological scenarios and an unknowable eschaton that is beyond the reach of analogy (and, hence, of eschatological verification). The former he renames *pareschatologies*. Hick sees pareschatologies as mythical expressions of eschatologies, which are transconceptual and transpersonal mysteries for which no analogies can be hypothesized, because they are "beyond human comprehension and expression" and transcend "the categories available [even] in our [spiritually] illumined thought and language" (*IR*, 347).

To put that differently: because eschatologies are beyond human comprehension, the human response to them is to develop pareschatological myths, which speak in human terms about something that, strictly speaking, cannot be referred to by any terms and that therefore is beyond the reach of all analogies (*IR*, 347, 355). Pareschatological myths are, in Hick's words, "imaginative pictures of the ultimate state produced to meet our need . . . for something to which our minds can cling as we contemplate our own finitude" (*IR*, 355). On this view, then, the pareschatological myths are modes of expression adapted to human needs and limits but that express nothing about transpersonal eschatological mysteries (*IR*, 355-56, 375).

At this point in his career, Hick claimed that only the pareschatologies are subject to verification, because analogies may be hypothesized between present existence and the pareschatological state. Hick doubted, however, that the pareschatologies are analogous to the eschatologies (a doubt that implies an *ultimate* denial of the validity of theological analogy) (*DEL*, 12, 22, 425). That is, human existence and expectation provide analogies of the intermediate postmortem pareschatologies, portrayed by the various religious traditions, although pareschatologies are not analogies of the ultimate eschatological states, which cannot be directly portrayed in any language. As Hick writes: "the subject matter of pareschatologies is less remote and may be less incommensurate with our present existence than that of the eschatologies" (*DEL*, 23).

On this approach, however, the eschatologies break the bond of analogy, while, paradoxically, the pareschatologies depend for their meaning upon the preservation of that bond. While an appeal to the distinction between eschatologies and pareschatologies gives hope of preserving the confirmability in principle of the intermediate pareschatologies, it actually negates them. The reason for this is that in the pareschatological state survivors would be in the same epistemological situation human beings are in presently—finite knowers with no sure criterion to determine whether what is encountered is that which would verify the claim that God exists. The situation is even worse with respect to eschatologies, since they cannot be spoken of with analogical but only with equivocal language.

This paradoxical situation, in which the pareschatologies make use of analogy merely in mirroring human expectations but become impotent equivocations when applied to eschatologies, nullifies the validity of Hick's proposal of eschatological verification. This failure impels Hick to begin developing a transcendent theological agnosticism, grounded in the distinction between noumena and phenomena, which Hick will eventually call the pluralistic hypothesis.[62] This move introduces an irresolvable dualism into Hick's philosophy of religions between an ineffable ultimate reality and human experience and language.

At first Hick tried to forestall the dualism to which his thought inescapably leads. At the end of *Death and Eternal Life*, despite his earlier recognition of the ineffableness of the eschaton, he claimed that the ultimate *eschatological* future is in fact personalistic and hence may best be represented analogically by the pareschatological myths of the theistic traditions. He suggested that

> our eschatological speculation terminates in the idea of the unity of mankind in a state in which the ego-aspect of individual consciousness has been left behind and the relational aspect has developed into a total community which is one-in-many and many-in-one, existing in a state which is probably not embodied and probably not in time (*DEL,* 464; see also 429-31).

This formulation, which owes much to the Hindu theistic philosopher Rāmānuja,[63] is an attempt to preserve the principle of analogy. The analogates in this case are finite human communities of persons-in-relation and the transcendent total community of persons-in-relation.

Given this analogy—which is consistent with personalist versions of theism—the possibility of eschatological verification would be preserved. However, it is preserved to the benefit of Hindu schools of philosophical theism and Christian philosophical theism and to the disadvantage of Advaita Vedānta and Buddhism, schools of thought in which an ultimate metaphysical personalism is denied. This quickly became an intolerable position for Hick, who wants to grant validity to the attempts of all (post-axial) religions to represent, despite their diversity, the ultimate truth of the divine reality.[64] Consequently, he dispenses with the metaphysical personalism of Rāmānuja and, as far as I can tell, never appeals to it again.

Myth Displaces Analogy

Hick began in the late seventies and early eighties to move toward his current position of holding that each of the *pareschatological* myths are analogies in their own local idioms of the unknowable, inexpressible (and, implicitly, nonanalogous) transpersonal Real *an sich*. He writes:

> Literal [i.e., factual] and analogical language about the objects of religious worship or meditation always intends to be about the Real itself [*an sich*]. And as such it functions mythologically: we speak mythologically about the noumenal Real by speaking literally or analogically about its phenomenal manifestations (*IR*, 351).

This distinction between mythological speech about the noumenal Real[65] and literal or analogical speech about the phenomenal manifestations of the Real is a new version of Hick's earlier distinction between eschatologies and pareschatologies. However, this new view explicitly dispenses with the notion of a factual or analogical *verificandum*, since the ineffable Real cannot be represented in factual (i.e., literalistic) propositions or in analogies, but can only be *aimed at* by myths. As construed by Hick, mythological speech includes what he once would have cited as examples of potentially verifiable, literal, or factual propositions. Theology is thus subordinated to mythology. He writes that mythological thought is not

> restricted to a narrative form. At a more abstract level there are philosophical and theological systems. . . . Examples are Hindu language concerning Brahman and the gods; Buddhist language concerning Sunyata and Trikaya; Christian language concerning the triune nature of God and the metaphysical attributes of God. [All of this] is mythological throughout in the sense that it constitutes human discourse about that which transcends the literal scope of human language (*IR*, 352).

At this point Hick has moved beyond the boundaries of verificationism. This does not constitute in Hick's view, however, an abandonment of his most central belief about religions, namely, that they have an inalienable cognitive dimension.[66] For even though religious discourse about metaphysical realities is mythological through and through, Hick does not think that this should reflect negatively upon the cognitivity of such discourse. He writes:

> The truthfulness or untruthfulness of mythological stories, images and conceptions does not consist in their literal adequacy to the nature of the Real *an sich*—in this respect it is not so much that they miss their target as that the target is totally beyond their range—but in their capacity to evoke appropriate or inappropriate dispositional responses to the Real [*an sich*] (*IR*, 353).

Rather than implying a rejection of religious cognitivity, this appeal to myth implies a differentiation of religious cognitivity from literalism, or verificationist factuality. Hick turns from analogy to myth in order to defend the transcendent and cognitivist intention of religious life and language. This way of viewing religious language and the question of its cognitivity marks a major change in Hick's understanding of the character of religious language. Hick now thinks that knowledge is acquired not only through logic and the study of nature (the only sources allowed by the verificationists) but also through *metaphor* (broadly conceived so as to include, as extended metaphors, religious myths, narratives, or stories, and conceptual systems). Unlike analogy or factual propositions, these metaphorical modes of speech, as construed by Hick, are equivocal forms of speech about the Real.

Thus, in the long quest for an ever more adequate conception of the *verificandum*, Hick is forced by the increasing futility of the task to give it up as impossible due to what appears to him to be the nonanalogous, or equivocal, character of the ultimate reality of which the various traditions speak. However, so as not to surrender what for him is the all-important belief that religions are cognitive, Hick must find a new way of conceiving religious cognitivity that is able to overcome the dualism of religious speech and the object of such speech implicit in the distinction between the ineffable noumenal Real and the mythological phenomena that are as-

42

cribed to it. This new way must also be able to overcome the circumstance that all speech about the noumenal Real must (in Hick's current understanding) be equivocal. This new way, to be explored at length in the next chapter, is Hick's quasi-Kantian pluralistic hypothesis, which depends upon the distinction between noumena and phenomena, and which employs the equivocal speech of mythology to speak about that which transcends all knowledge and experience.

Notes

[1] Simply stated, the pluralistic hypothesis, involves the claim that all post-axial religions equally represent the noumenal Real. Hick distinguishes between pre-axial religions (prior to the first millennium BCE), which were concerned with preserving the cosmic and social order, and post-axial religions, which are concerned with the individual's quest for salvation or liberation (*IR*, 22–29). Hick is concerned only with the latter forms of religion in the pluralistic hypothesis.

[2] *Verificandum:* "that which is to be verified," or the experience, should it occur, that would verify the assertion that God exists. Hick uses the term in *PRP*, 116.

[3] In the introduction to "Theology and Verification," Hick makes clear what he wants to do in this article: to take "the verification principle in modified form and [try] to show that 'God exists' is (whether true or false) a genuinely factual assertion" (*EG*, 252; see also 267–68).

[4] For major formulations of this proposal see the following writings of Hick. Early versions of the proposal occur in "Theology and Verification" (*EG*, 252–74); *FK1*, 145–63; *CC*, 99–106; *PR2*, 90–96; "Comment on Luther J. Binkley's 'What Characterizes Religious Language?'," *Journal for the Scientific Study of Religion* 2 (1962): 22–24; "A Comment on Professor Binkley's Reply," *Journal for The Scientific Study of Religion* 2 (1963): 231–32; "Sceptics and Believers," *FP*, 235–50. Later versions of the proposal occur in *FK2*, 169–99; *PRP*, 110–24; *DEL*, 25. The most recent versions occur in *PRP*, 124–25; *IR*, 13, 177–88, 356, 371, 375; *WBG*, 32, 45.

[5] Luther J. Binkley, "What Characterizes Religious Language?" *Journal for the Scientific Study of Religion* 2 (1962): 230; Terry Richard Mathis, *Against John Hick* (Boston: University Press of America, 1985), 117.

[6] Hick writes: "Now although we cannot look into the minds of the seminal religious thinkers of the past, or the body of believers from century to century within the great traditions, it nevertheless seems to me transparently evident that they

have normally understood their own and one another's core language in a realist way.... That God-talk has normally been construed cognitively is clear from the ways in which it has connected with speakers' emotions and modes of behaviour... . when in response to the language of their scriptures, liturgies, and creeds theistic believers address God in prayer; look about to see if their prayers are being answered; receive calamities as God's punishment and well-being as an expression of divine favour; are in fear of hell and in hope of heaven; feel guilty, forgiven, thankful in relation to God; or even, as in ancient days, sacrifice human lives to their gods, we properly attribute to them a realist interpretation of the realm of language in which they are participating. A non-realist interpretation is, in contrast, radically revisionary.... But despite the failure of some [theologians] to acknowledge this it seems to me abundantly clear that the core of religious language has normally been understood by believers and disbelievers alike as basically cognitive" (IR, 176–77). In Hick's view, revisionary nonrealist theologians, such as Don Cupitt and D. Z. Phillips, are unintentional elitists (207), since their interpretation of religion "constitutes bad news for all except a fortunate minority" (205). Only a fortunate few human beings have had the privilege of realizing "an eternal quality of existence in this life" (206). Unfortunately, the great majority of human beings who have ever lived have died with "their highest potentialities unfulfilled—and if the non-realists are right, permanently and irrevocably unfulfilled. This would negate any notion of the ultimate goodness of the universe" (207). Here we see a fundamental motive underlying Hick's defense of the cognitivity of religion, a concern that he shares with Kant, the Biblical writers, and thinkers in almost all religious traditions—with all who have intuited, even in the absence of good arguments, the existence of some sort of future life where justice and mercy must prevail if the vast display of human folly and the otherwise irrevocable anguish and loss that marks so many lives are not to be the last word about the human race.

[7] In his 1981 Gifford Lectures, Seyyed Hossein Nasr eloquently defended this traditional view: "In the Orient knowledge has always been related to the sacred and to spiritual perfection. To know has ultimately meant to be transformed by the very process of knowing, as the Western tradition was to assert over the ages before it was eclipsed by the postmedieval secularization and humanization that forced the separation of knowing from being and intelligence. The Oriental sage has always embodied spiritual perfection; intelligence has been seen ultimately as a sacrament, and knowledge has been irrevocably related to the sacred and its actualization in the being of the knower. And this relation continues wherever and whenever the tradition still survives despite all the vicissitudes of the modern world" (Knowledge and the Sacred [Edinburgh: Edinburgh University Press, 1981], vi–viii).

[8] Hick later offered a quite different definition of cognitive, one that is designed to

circumvent the impediments to the defense of theological cognitivity conceived in verificationist terms.

9 R. W. Ashby, *The Encyclopedia of Philosophy*, s.v. "verifiability principle"; Hilary Putnam, *Philosophical Papers* (New York: Cambridge University Press, 1983), vol. 3, *Realism and Reason*, 27–28.

10 For other formulations of Hick's version of the verification principle, see *EG*, 254, 259; "A Comment on Professor Binkley's Reply," 231-232; *FP*, 249; *CC*, 99-100; *PRP*, 113; *IR*, 177. Hick's version of the principle is a late, liberal version that was apparently forged with Herbert Feigl's modest verification principle in mind (*PRP*, 113-114). Feigl's version of the principle required that a meaningful statement just be confirmable in principle. This version of the verification principle is broad enough so as not to exclude all the statements that science wants to keep, yet only excludes hypotheses that are "immune against tests of even the most indirect sort," such as absolute space and time, the phlogiston, the ether, vital forces, and so forth (Herbert Feigl, "Some Major Issues and Developments in the Philosophy of Science of Logical Empiricism," in *The Foundations of Science and the Concepts of Psychology and Psychoanalysis*, ed. Herbert Feigl and Michael Scriven [Minneapolis: Minnesota University Press, 1956], 15). Purged from Feigl's liberal verificationism is the virulent antitheological animus of the early verificationist movement—as mordantly expressed, for example, in A. J. Ayer's widely influential *Language, Truth and Logic*, 2d ed. (1946; reprint, New York: Dover, 1952), 113-120. Feigl's latitudinarian verificationism is, by his own account, able to accommodate *inductive* metaphysics and natural theology (by *natural theology* I take Feigl to mean variations on teleological arguments, not the a priori arguments), though it would still outlaw *transcendent* metaphysics and *transcendent* theology. Consequently, he can assert that there is no clear line of demarcation between science and *inductive* metaphysics (or even between the former and *natural* theology [Feigl, "Some Major Issues and Developments in the Philosophy of Science of Logical Empiricism," 15]). Feigl's concessions are all that an empirical theologian or philosopher of religion could ask from the philosopher of science, since the *empirical* theologian (including Hick at this point in his career) is concerned with justifying inductively or observationally verifiable statements about God and is usually as much opposed to transcendent theology (which relies upon the a priori arguments) as is the empirical philosopher. Thus, in spite of his positivistic background, which made him "somewhat allergic to the term 'metaphysics'," Feigl came to see that this word can "cover quite respectable or at least semirespectable endeavors" (Feigl, 22). So much did his new respect for the word grow, that he allowed that scientists are "inductive metaphysicians" and even logical empiricists are metaphysicians of a sort, though certainly not intuitive, transcendent, a priori, or dialectical metaphysicians (Feigl, 22).

11 See also Hick, "A Comment on Professor Binkley's Reply," 231.

[12] Hick elaborates this point: "I want to suggest that the Christian belief in the reality of God . . . is—whether true or false—a genuinely factual belief. It is not empirical, if the empirical realm is confined by definition to the material universe. But it is factual if we use this as a wider term than 'empirical' and define the factual in terms of making an actual or possible difference within human experience" (FP, 249). See also "A Comment on Professor Binkley's Reply," where Hick also claims that the 'factual' is wider than the 'empirical'. He then goes on to say that "I should define 'fact' in terms of 'making an actual or possible experienceable difference,' and should wish to allow experience to show what various kinds of facts there are. It would, I think, be dogmatism of the most unproductive kind to stipulate that if we enjoy experiences after death the realm of existence which is thus experienced is not to count as fact. (Even so orthodox a logical positivist as Moritz Schlick acknowledged that 'survival of death' constitutes a testable hypothesis, although it is one that cannot be tested without dying" (231). As pointed out by Virgil C. Aldrich, Schlick's view of the possibility of verification of immortality is based on the contention that, in Aldrich's words, "what is imaginable is verifiable in principle, hence perhaps factually significant" ("Messrs. Schlick and Ayer on Immortality," in *Readings in Philosophical Analysis*, ed. Herbert Feigl and Wilfrid Sellars [New York: Appleton-Century-Crofts, 1949], 173). Aldrich characterizes Schlick's position as coming from the 'rightist' wing of logical analysis, which is opposed by the 'leftist' wing of Carnap and Ayer. Significantly for the present discussion, Aldrich points out that one of the issues separating these two camps (at least when Aldrich was writing in 1938) concerns the role that the logically possible or imaginable plays in the theory of meaning: "Schlick's broader conception of what can be experienced is more in accord with actual linguistic usage or convention, but . . . this stand of his is an unconsciously camouflaged departure from the *positivistic* principle of empirical verifiability and meaning. On the other hand, Ayer's narrower conception of the empirical, truer though it be to radical phenomenalism and radical conventionalism, and more rigorously formulated than Schlick's, makes nonsense of much of what is *imaginable* in the ordinary sense. And since what can be imagined is very commonly recognized as empirically *significant* though not always *true*, Ayer should either (1) give us better proof that we cannot really imagine such states of affairs as being immortal, or (2) prove that imagination is not sufficient for empirical meaning contrary to general belief, or (3) show that some imaginable states of affairs are empirically significant and others, such as immortality, not" ("Messrs. Schlick and Ayer on Immortality," 174).

[13] This view is also held by Antony Flew and Alasdair MacIntyre in their co-edited volume *New Essays in Philosophical Theology* (1955; reprint, London: SCM Press, 1963), viii, ix. This volume contains many of the important articles that were inspired by "Gods." Some of these essays were again reprinted along with later articles, including Hick's own *locus classicus* in this debate, "Theology and

Verification," in Hick, *EG*, 217–98. Many of these articles, as well as newer essays on the topic of verificationism and theology, can be found in *The Logic of God: Theology and Verificationism*, ed. Malcolm L. Diamond and Thomas V. Litzenburg, Jr. (Indianapolis: Bobbs-Merrill Company, 1975).

[14] John Wisdom, "Gods," in *Classical and Contemporary Readings in the Philosophy of Religion*, 3rd ed., ed. John Hick (Englewood Cliffs, NJ: Prentice-Hall, 1990 [article originally published in 1944]), 338–39.

[15] Antony Flew, "Theology and Falsification," in *EG*, 224–28.

[16] Flew, "Theology and Falsification," in *EG*, 225.

[17] This approach fails to take into account Hans Reichenbach's argument that the equivalence of testable consequences does not necessarily imply cognitive equivalence. See appendix.

[18] Flew, "Theology and Falsification," in *EG*, 227.

[19] John Hick, "Straightening the Record: Some Responses to Critics," *Modern Theology* 7 (1990): 193.

[20] However, the theist may claim that the evidence appealed to by theists and nontheists *is not the same*, for some theists may accept various paranormal events, such as healings, divine interventions, answers to prayer, and mystical experiences, as evidential. Thus, it is highly controversial to claim that the evidence for both positions is the same, for this claim implies the acceptance of the standards of a narrowly circumscribed scientific mentality as the final standard of evidence. Hick, as is evident from his own parable, loses a great deal of potential evidence for theism by accepting the claim that at least in this life the evidence *is* the same and that therefore the issue at stake between the theist and the nontheist is not *in via*, at present, experimental. What is crucial for Hick is the possibility of a future confirmation *in patria* (i.e., in heaven, or in the eschatological Kingdom of God) of the claim that God exists after death.

[21] Perhaps the analysis of testable equivalence provided in the appendix could show Hick a way out of his uncritical acceptance of the belief that there is no way at present to decide conclusively between theistic and atheistic interpretations of the same evidence.

[22] Hick does not naively assume that God *will* be encountered in an afterdeath state. The mere logical possibility of such an encounter is sufficient to insure the meaningfulness, or potential verifiability, of the claim that God exists. The truth or falsity of the claim is another matter entirely, and, regardless of the outcome, the claim remains meaningful. Hick's position does not imply that there *is* a future life, but only that the possibility that there may be one—and it cannot be ruled out as a logical possibility—makes the theistic claim factually meaningful by offering possible evidence that would show that theism and its negation will not be testably

equivalent hypotheses in a logically possible afterdeath state (for more about testable equivalence, see the appendix). Eschatological verification thus confers factual status upon theistic or religious claims by suggesting the idea of a *possible* life to come in which God is sufficiently well encountered so as to decide the issue between theism and atheism conclusively; it is not, however, the claim that such a life is *actual* or *will* be the case. Of course, it may turn out that at death we are totally annihilated, and so no verification or falsification of any eschatological claim could occur. Or we may survive and falsify "God exists" by encountering an absolutely evil being (*FK1*, 156).

[23] An earlier, though subsequently abandoned, attempt to develop a cognitivist approach to defend religion against the challenge of Wisdom's and Flew's parables was that of Ian Crombie, whose "postponement of verification to the hereafter" (Ronald W. Hepburn, *Christianity and Paradox: Critical Studies in Twentieth-Century Theology* [London: Watts, 1958], 14) is based on the claim that dying is the test that allows religious utterances to be placed within the logical classification of the statement of facts (I. M. Crombie, "Theology and Falsification," in Flew and MacIntyre, *New Essays in Philosophical Theology*, 126, 129). Hick would have agreed with Crombie, but wanted to go further. Hick *denies* that the mere survival of death, should it occur, would constitute a confirmation of the claim that God exists. As he writes: "So far I have argued that a survival prediction such as is contained in the *corpus* of Christian belief is in principle subject to future verification. But this does not take the argument by any means as far as it must go if it is to succeed. For survival, simply as such, would not serve to verify theism. It would not necessarily be a state of affairs which is manifestly incompatible with the non-existence of God. It might just be taken as a surprising natural fact. The atheist, in his resurrection body, and able to remember his life on earth, might say that the universe has turned out to be more complex, and perhaps more to be approved of, than he had realized. But the mere fact of survival, with a new body in a new environment, would not demonstrate to him that there is a God. It is fully compatible with the notion of survival that the life to come be, so far as the theistic problem is concerned, essentially a continuation of the present life, and religiously no less ambiguous. And in this event, survival after bodily death would not in the least constitute a final verification of theistic faith" (*EG*, 267–68). Moritz Schlick would have agreed with Hick at least as far as the *meaningfulness* of the survival claim is concerned, as Hick notes (*EG*, 262). Schlick wrote, on the basis of the strictest notion of verification, in which meaning is identical with an empirical operation, that "we must conclude that immortality . . . should not be regarded as a 'metaphysical problem,' but is an empirical hypothesis, because it possesses logical verifiability. It could be verified by following the prescription: 'Wait until you die!' The hypothesis of immortality is an empirical statement which owes its meaning to its verifiability, and it has no meaning beyond its possibility of verification" ("Meaning and Verification," in Feigl and

Sellars, *Readings in Philosophical Analysis*, 160). Even if the proposal of eschatological verification will not be applicable to the question of God's existence in the afterdeath state, it retain significance insofar as it keeps open the possibility of verifying *the survival of death*. For to find oneself alive in any form after the death of one's body constitutes a verification of a religious over against a reductionistic monistic materialist doctrine, which denies survival because of the supposed rigid identity of mind and body, implying that whatever is spiritual or mental in the individual dies with the death of the cells of the nervous system. On this point, Hick writes, "if there is a further development of human experience, beyond the present life, which is incompatible with a naturalistic understanding of the universe but which develops and enlarges our various religious understandings of it, this will constitute verification of the religious side of the religious/naturalistic opposition" (*PRP*, 125; see also *IR*, 13, 356). Thus, the mere survival of death, should it occur, would confirm the validity of the religious perspective in general, since survival would invalidate the belief that individual human existence is limited to the confines the physical body. Thus, one may imagine A. J. Ayer in the afterlife pleasantly surprised to find himself in such a place after all, but not thereby any more disposed to assent to statements about a divine being.

[24] In *PRP*, 125–26 n. 7, Hick gives bibliographic information on the major interpretive articles and sections of books where interpretations of eschatological verification have been proposed This list ends at 1977 and leaves out what is probably the first response to eschatological verification: W. E. Kennick's review of *FK1* in *Philosophical Review* 57 (1958): 407–409. In this review, Kennick lampoons eschatological verification as a "bizarre device." While most interpretations of Hick in recent years have focused upon his Copernican theology of religions and his pluralistic hypothesis in the philosophy of religions, a number of works treating eschatological verification have also appeared, such as: Frederick Sontag, "Anselm and the Concept of God," *Scottish Journal of Theology* 35 (1982): 213–16; Mathis, *Against John Hick* (1985); Beth Mackie, "Concerning 'Eschatological Verification Reconsidered,'" *Religious Studies* 23 (1987): 129–35.

[25] Plato called analogy "the most beautiful of all bonds" (*desmōn kallistos*) in *Timaeus*, 31c. This translation of the Greek phrase can be found in *Sacramentum Mundi*, s.v. "analogy of being."

[26] Norbert W. Mtega, *Analogy and Theological Language in the* Summa Contra Gentiles: *A Textual Survey of the Concept of Analogy and its Theological Application by St. Thomas* (Frankfurt Am Main: Peter Lang, 1984), 31–32, 87. Classic modern works on theological analogy are Hampus Lyttkens, *The Analogy between God and the World: An Investigation of its Background and Interpretation of its Use by Thomas of Aquino* (Uppsala: Almqvist & Wiksells Boktrycckeri AB, 1952) and George P. Klubertanz, *St. Thomas on Analogy: A Textual and Systematic Synthesis* (Chicago: Loyola University Press, 1960). Recent studies in which the issue of

theological analogy is taken up include Frederick M. Jelly, "The Relationship Between Symbolic and Literary Language about God, in *Naming God*, Robert P. Scharlemann, ed. (New York: Paragon House, 1985), 52–64, and David Burrell, *Knowing the Unknowable God: Ibn-Sina, Maimonides, Aquinas* (Notre Dame: University of Notre Dame Press, 1986). Included in this list should be the less recent but still useful studies by Herbert McCabe and Victor Preller that are cited in later footnotes.

[27] Thomas Aquinas *Summa Theologiae* 1a. 13. 5, *responsio* (trans. McCabe, 3.64).

[28] Herbert McCabe's commentary on his translation of Thomas Aquinas, *Summa Theologiae* (New York: Blackfriars/McGraw-Hill, 1964), vol. 3, *Knowing and Naming God*, 109.

[29] The doctrine of analogy may be criticized on the grounds that it involves an illicit use of the concept of cause: it involves reference to a transcendent, eminent cause of created qualities such as *good, wise*, etc., even though, as Kant argued, the concept of cause cannot be so invoked. As Kant argued: "all laws regulating the transition from effects to cause, all synthesis and extension of our knowledge, refer to nothing but possible experience, and therefore solely to objects of the sensible world, and apart from them can have no meaning whatsoever" (*Critique of Pure Reason*, trans. Norman Kemp Smith [New York: St. Martin's Press, 1965], A622/ B650). In the same vein, Victor Preller complains about the "horrendously naive attempts [of Thomists] to explicate the relation between 'God' and 'the world.' Most of this nonsense parades under the name of 'analogy'. . . . I shall simply outline the basic circularity of the all-too-popular move—a circularity which affects almost all attempts to specify in intelligible terms the relation between the logic of 'God' and the logic of 'things in the world.' The normal move is to begin with the claim that God is the 'cause' of the world. On the basis of that relation, it is believed possible to predicate certain 'perfections' of God in a mode appropriate to the 'cause' of the world—the 'first cause,' as it is called. To exhibit the circularity of the move, we must immediately challenge the use of 'cause' in relation to God. If we ask how the Thomist is using 'cause' he normally replies in terms of 'efficient causality'—that mode of causing a thing which explains that a thing is. In common terms God is the 'maker' or 'creator' of the world. The non-Thomist is likely to reply that he is only familiar with uses of 'causing,' 'making,' or 'creating' which refer to ordinary occurrences *within* the world" (*Divine Science: A Reformulation of Thomas Aquinas* [Princeton: Princeton University Press, 1967], 19–20). Another criticism is that analogy is redundant. That is, since one cannot establish the principle of analogy by way of analogy alone, an independent ground is required to verify that the analogates (God and creatures) are related analogically. But if there is such a ground—revelation, for instance—appeal to analogy becomes redundant (Frederick Ferré, *Language, Logic, and God*, [1961; reprint, New York: Harper and Row, 1969], 74). Ferré takes his stance here from

Dorothy M. Emmet, *The Nature of Metaphysical Thinking* (London: Macmillan, 1945), 180. An even more damaging charge against analogy is that it is "excessively permissive," in that it allows no control over what predicates, derived from creatures, may be applied to God. As Ferré asks: "can the theist be content to admit a method of talking which would seem to make God 'sweet tasting' as well as 'good,' 'finely powdered' as well as 'wise'?" (*Language, Logic, and God*, 74). See footnote 38 for another criticism of theological analogy by Ferré.

[30] David B. Burrell, *Knowing the Unknowable God*, 3.

[31] Thomas Aquinas *Summa Theologiae* 1a. 13. 2, *responsio* (trans. Dominican Fathers, 1.61).

[32] Herbert McCabe, *Summa Theologiae*, vol. 3: 107.

[33] As Thomas wrote: "Though God is wholly simple we must still address him with a multitude of names. Our mind is not able to grasp his essence. We have to start from the things about us, which have diverse perfections though their root and origin in God is one. Because we cannot name objects except in the way we understand them, for words are the signs of concepts, we can name God only from the terms employed elsewhere. These are manifold, therefore we must make use of many terms. Were we to see God in himself we would not call on a multitude of words; our knowledge would be as simple as his nature is simple. We look forward to this in the day of our glory; *in that day there shall be one Lord and his name one*" (Zach. 14:9). St. Thomas Aquinas Opusc. XII *Compendium Theologiae*, 24. Translated by Thomas Gilby, *Saint Thomas Aquinas: Philosophical Texts* (New York: Oxford University Press, 1951), §199.

[34] Thomas Aquinas *Summa Theologiae* 1a. 13. 6, *responsio* (trans. Dominican Fathers, 1.65).

[35] Burrell, *Knowing the Unknowable God*, 53.

[36] An appeal to analogy is implicit in Hick's first formulation of eschatological verification. Rejecting the possibility of a direct vision of God, he proposes that the possible future life will be "a situation that points unambiguously to the existence of a loving God" (*EG*, 268). Present existence is ambiguous on this point, Hick claims. He goes on to claim that our awareness of this ambiguity presupposes that we "already have some idea, however vague, of what it would be for our situation to be not ambiguous, but on the contrary wholly evidential of God" (269). But because God is infinite and we are finite, we cannot recognize God directly as being *perfect* goodness, love, and so forth: "such qualities cannot be given in human experience" (270). Consequently, "one cannot claim to have encountered a Being whom one recognized to be the infinite, almighty, eternal Creator" (271). However, this consequence threatens to undermine eschatological verification, which depends for its meaningfulness upon the possibility of confirming in a hypothetical afterdeath state that God exists. Hick's first attempt at an answer to this

problem is an appeal to Jesus Christ and the Incarnation. This move will be discussed presently in the body of this chapter.

[37] See *IR*, 176, 247, where Hick uses the term *analogous* in Thomas' sense.

[38] Ferré criticizes the theological usefulness of analogy precisely on this point: "It would appear impossible in principle that any finite characteristic could be identical with an infinite characteristic. If there is to be a relation of identity of abstractable characteristics between man and God, either man's finitude or God's infinitude is sure to be violated. . . . It is no longer possible, I believe, to hold that the logic of analogy, as it has normally been interpreted, is cogent" (*Language, Logic, and God*, 76).

[39] Gavin D'Costa, *John Hick's Theology of Religions: A Critical Evaluation* (Lanham, MD: University Press of America, 1987), 170–78.

[40] This version of eschatological verification uses terms that are subservient to the sensory parameters of a rather crude empiricism, which shares a common theoretical lineage with the Baconian literalism of fundamentalism. On the latter, see George M. Marsden, *Fundamentalism and American Culture: The Shaping of Twentieth-Century Evangelicalism, 1870–1925* (New York: Oxford University Press, 1980), 7, 15, 19, 55–62. Victor Kraft, an early historian of the Vienna Circle and logical positivism, cogently summarizes the empiricist outlook: "The given constitutes the basis of all word-meanings; this is a central thesis of empiricism. Meanings must ultimately be founded upon presentation of the designated, and therefore all meanings must ultimately be reducible to the given, which alone is capable of presentation. And this means that all conceptual meanings can be constructed on the basis of experienced data alone" (*The Vienna Circle: The Origin of Neo-Positivism*, trans. A. Pap [1953; reprint, New York: Greenwood Press, 1969], 84). I think that the younger Hick would have found very little to disagree with in this way of putting the matter.

[41] As evidence of how far Hick has traveled from his earlier literalism, Hick wrote in 1989: "The answers of the religious traditions, if construed as literal factual hypotheses, are manifestly inadequate. But I want to suggest that if understood mythologically they may do something to orient us towards the Real whilst at the same time assuaging our anxiety in face of the deep mystery of our existence" (*IR*, 356).

[42] Hick does allude generally to this issue in *FK1*, where he points out that unless God is embodied "it is not evident how he might be visible to embodied beings" in the eschatological kingdom (159). This statement indicates a startling literalism and physicalism, although it has the virtue of being consistent with the literalistic and physicalistic views of the resurrection still held and vigorously defended by conservative evangelical Christians and fundamentalists. For an example of how an atheistic physicalism and a fundamentalist Christian physicalism coincide, see

Gary Habermas and Antony Flew, *Did Jesus Rise from the Dead? The Resurrection Debate* (San Francisco: Harper and Row, 1987). In setting up the debate, Flew points out that both he and Gary Habermas agree on the meaning of the resurrection: "we both construe *resurrection*, or rising from the dead, in a thoroughly literal and physical way" (3). They disagree, however, over whether the event happened or was even possible. Habermas, a professor at Jerry Falwell's Liberty University, claims that it was possible and did happen; Flew takes the opposite view.

[43] Or as Thomas Aquinas explains the ultimate endstate: "Were we to see God in himself we would not call on a multitude of words; our knowledge would be as simple as his nature is simple. We look forward to this in the day of our glory; *in that day there shall be one Lord and his name one*" (Zach. 14.9). St. Thomas Aquinas Opusc. XIII *Compendium Theologiae* 24 (Gilby, *Saint Thomas Aquinas: Philosophical Texts* §199).

[44] That is, human life in its naturally evolved body (carbon-based), in a cybernetic prosthetic body (silicon-based—a bit of scientific fantasy seriously proposed by the astronomer Robert Jastrow, among others), or in a resurrection body (spirit-based—see 1 Cor. 15:42–49).

[45] As A. W. Moore writes: "I cannot receive the metaphysically infinite whole. This is because my own finitude sets limits on how much I can take in, and how much I can be affected by what is out there. It is as if my reception is itself a kind of conditioning. If I were going to receive that which was complete, absolute, self-explanatory, and independent of all else, and if I were going to be aware of it as such, I should myself have to become infinite. I should have to be 'absorbed' into the infinite, and lose my (finite) self in it. Hegel believed that this was exactly the kind of thing that was destined to happen" (*The Infinite* [New York: Routledge, 1990], 219).

[46] This move seems to involve a Barthian rejection of the Thomist *analogia entis* for what Barth called the *analogia fidei*. Emil Brunner, however, forcefully exposed the incoherence of this move: "This is the place for a few words concerning the principle of analogy and Barth's polemic against it. Barth is the first theologian to see in the use of the principle of analogy a—or even *the*—contrast between Protestantism and Roman Catholicism. For Barth holds the strange doctrine that there is no creature which has in itself a likeness to God. Rather it is raised to this status by the revelation in Christ and through the Holy Spirit. This is a piece of theological nominalism, in comparison with which that of William of Occam appears harmless. For this would mean that we call God 'Father,' 'Son,' 'Spirit,' that we speak of the 'Word' of God, etc., not because God is more like a father than anything else, but simply because God says so in the Scriptures. God does not say it because by his creation and from his creation it is so, but on the contrary, it only becomes so by the Word of God in Scripture [*analogia fidei*]. In fact and in truth

Barth is not able to maintain this extreme nominalism consistently. Barth's *Dogmatics*, like all others, are of course based on the idea of analogy [*analogia entis*], even though he does not acknowledge this" (Karl Brunner and Karl Barth, *Natural Theology*, trans. Peter Fraenkel [London: Geoffrey Bles: The Centenary Press, 1946], 53–54).

[47] Hick introduces this classic terminology in *EG*, 261 to refer to the Christian's earthly sojourn and the Christian's life in her spiritual homeland, the Kingdom of God.

[48] Hick briefly acknowledged this problem in *EG*, 272, where he wonders whether the New Testament gives a sufficiently authentic picture of Jesus Christ to make recognition of him possible. Nevertheless, turning away from this exegetical issue, he claims in this early essay (1960) that the logical point remains the same: "a verification of theism . . . is dependent upon the Christian's having a genuine contact with the person of Christ, even though this is mediated through the life and tradition of the Church."

[49] 1 Cor. 2:9 NIV.

[50] Writing in 1977, Hick rejected his claim in *EG* that we will know that we have encountered the infinite God, because we will encounter Jesus, who is "the knowability of God" (271). He now no longer thinks of Jesus "as the one and only revelation of God" and no longer wants "to treat [Jesus'] teaching as our sole source of knowledge of God's nature" (*PRP*, 121).

[51] Not even observing Jesus *in patria* would be essential to eschatological verification, since instead of any recognizable form of Jesus, the believer might encounter the supreme instance of divinity as Kṛṣṇa playing his flute, or as a Buddha or Buddhess inviting one into a Pure Land. Influenced by encounters with other religions, Hick thus rejects the belief that Jesus Christ is the only way to God *in via* or *in patria* (*PRP*, 121).

[52] For examples of this *complex* verificandum, see *PRP*, 100, where Hick suggests "a more probable 'eschatological scenario' . . . in which we move in [postmortem] stages towards the ultimate relationship or to union with the divine, and that as we approach nearer to the consummation our conceptions of 'how things are' will gradually become more adequate. It seems likely that in this process many of the ideas embedded within each of the religious traditions will become variously modified or marginalised or superseded." Hick worked out this "eschatological scenario" in great detail in *DEL* (chapter 20 ff.), which was published the same year as "Eschatological Verification Reconsidered" (reprinted in *PRP*, 110–28). Hick returned to these ideas in "A Possible Conception of Life After Death," in *Death and Afterlife*, ed. Stephen T. Davis (New York: St. Martin's Press, 1989), 183–95.

[53] On the other hand, the effacing and final sublation of personhood over a series

of lives into an impersonal divine reality or the termination of personhood at the death of the body would invalidate eschatological verification and the principle of analogy, which underlies it.

[54] The development in Hick's views of eschatological verification can be reckoned chronologically and theologically, with the latter being a better guide, since Hick's writings of many periods have frequently been reprinted, sometimes updated and sometimes not. He himself often takes over whole passages almost verbatim from earlier writings (for instance, the inserting of most of "Theology and Verification" into *FK2* as chapter eight). Theologically, the doctrine of eschatological verification changes insofar as Hick's theology changes from an orthodox Christocentric theism (fifties to late sixties), to a pluralistic Copernican theism (early seventies to late seventies), and, most recently, to the pluralistic post-Christian, post-theistic doctrine of the Real *an sich* (which will be discussed in the next chapter). This development occurs in response to criticisms of earlier versions of eschatological verification and also as a result of Hick's own increasing awareness of the plurality and irreconcilable diversity of the claims of the various religious traditions.

[55] As Hick attempts in *IR*, 180–83.

[56] The elusiveness of the eschatological *verificandum* is due both to the mystery of ultimate human destiny—a mystery that eludes analogies even while teasingly encouraging the making of them—and to the plurality of diverse eschatological scenarios offered by the world religions.

[57] Advaita Vedānta is a Hindu philosophical school espousing nondualism (i.e., an immaterial radical monism), which was most brilliantly defended by Śankara (c. 788–820).

[58] Gauḍapāda, one of Śankara's predecessors, taught the doctrine of *ajātivāda*: "No *Jīva* is ever born. There does not exist any cause which can produce it. This is the highest Truth that nothing is ever born [*ajāti*]." Since neither the individual being (*jīva*) nor, as Śankara points out in his commentary on this passage, the means to the attaining of *mokṣa* have ever existed, these notions are meaningless from the ultimate standpoint of *nirguṇa* Brahman (*The Māndūkya Upaniṣad with Gauḍapāda's and Śankara's Commentary*, 5th ed., trans. Swami Nikhilananda [Calcutta: Advaita Ashrama, 1987], 210-11). Consequently, Hick fails in his attempt to extend eschatological verification to *mokṣa*. Arvind Sharma undertakes to harmonize Hick's view on this point with Advaita Vedānta in *The Philosophy of Religion and Advaita Vedānta: A Comparative Study in Religion and Reason* (University Park, PA: The Pennsylvania State University Press, 1995), 152–167.

[59] There are theistic schools of Vedānta, as seen in the case of Rāmānuja (11th century), who would vigorously disagree with the nondualist (*advaita*) view of Brahman advocated by Śankara. Rāmānuja's version of Vedānta is called

viśiṣṭādvaita, or modified nondualism, the basic principle of which is identity-in-difference (*bhedābheda*), rather than pure identity (or unmodified nonduality—*advaita*). In these theistic schools, analogy would take precedence over equivocation.

[60] This issue arises in the New Testament, as evidenced by the use of *we* to refer to Christians in the eschatological encounter with the infinite reality of God, even though it is not clear what *we* will signify at that point: "Beloved, we are God's children now; it does not yet appear what we shall be, but we know that when he appears we shall be like him, for we shall see him as he is" (I John 3:2 RSV).

[61] Hick admits that the claims of other religions make it increasingly difficult to say *what* will constitute a verification (for Hinduism, see *IR*, 180–83; for Buddhism, 183–84, 187); nevertheless, his basic argument for the cognitivity of these eschatological scenarios remains the same (180–86). However, Michael Tooley, a critic of Hick, writes, "when theological statements are interpreted as purporting to refer to something that transcends the realm of human experience, appeal to eschatological verification does not even show *that* theological statements have factual content, let alone provide an adequate account of *what* their factual content is" ("John Hick and the Concept of Eschatological Verification," *Religious Studies* 12 [1976], 84).

[62] John Hick, "Mystical Experience as Cognition," in *Understanding Mysticism*, ed. Richard Woods (Garden City, NY: Doubleday, 1980), 429. This article was written in the same year that *DEL* appeared—1976—though it was not published until 1980.

[63] The Hindu (or, more precisely, the Śrī Vaiṣṇava) theologian, philosopher and Vedāntic commentator Rāmānuja taught the doctrine of *viśiṣṭādvaita*, or qualified nondualism, which allows for the distinction between God and individual beings to be maintained. This view is offered as a challenge to the nondualist Advaita philosophy of Śaṅkara, which sublates such distinctions altogether. Thus, in contrast to Śaṅkara, who taught the nondual, or monistic, doctrine that individuals are really identical with and only illusorily distinct from Brahman, or the Absolute, Rāmānuja modified this relationship by holding that human individuals and Brahman are really simultaneously identical *and* nonidentical. Śaṅkara's doctrine undermines the ultimacy of real, distinct persons, while Rāmānuja's supports it. The former doctrine cannot be made to support theism in a sense acceptable to classical Christianity, while the latter can.

[64] This, after all, is the point of Hick's so-called Copernican revolution in theology. First presented in his 1972 Carrs Lane Lectures (*GUF*, chapter 9), this revolution calls for the rejection in religion of the "Ptolemaic" standpoint, which involves "the conviction that one's own religion is at the center of the religious universe and provides a touchstone for the truth of all other world faiths" (*DEL*,

30). In place of this standpoint, Hick calls for a religious Copernican revolution, which places not this or that religion but the Ultimate Reality aimed at by all of the religions at the center of the universe of faiths. Thus, neither Christ, God, Buddha, Allah, Brahman, nor *Dharmadhātu* is the Ultimate Reality itself. On the contrary, each of these ought to be seen as mythological "responses to variously overlapping aspects of the same Ultimate Reality" (31). While providing validity to each of these mythological pictures as responses to Ultimate Reality, this does not mean that Hick claims that all religions are *equally* valid. He writes that "if we think for a moment of the entire range of religious phenomena, no one is going to maintain that they are all on the same level of value or validity" (*PRP*, 67; see also Anne Hunt, "No Other Name? A Critique of Religious Pluralism," *Pacifica* 3 [1990], 54 n. 27).

[65] Hick interchanges the phrases *the noumenal Real* and *the Real* an sich (for the former use, see *IR*, 246). I will generally use the former, more euphonious phrase in place of the more cumbersome latter phrase.

[66] As late as 1989, Hick still maintained a realist view of religion that holds to an enduring principle that was central to outmoded logical positivsim, namely, "the basic empiricist principle that to exist is to make an in-principle experienceable difference" in the world, a principle that can still be applied eschatologically to soteriologically orienting myths (reply to Chester Gillis in *Problems in the Philosophy of Religion: Critical Studies of the Work of John Hick*, ed. Harold Hewitt, Jr. (New York: St. Martin's Press, 1991), 51-52.

3

The Pluralistic Hypothesis

The problem of conceiving the nature of the eschatological *verificandum*, especially as exacerbated by the diversity and mutual incompatibility of the ultimate claims and mythologies of the religions, gradually impelled Hick to reject the verificationist identification of cognitivity with factuality. Coupled with this rejection is Hick's recasting of his notion of religious cognitivity. Now he contends that the truthfulness of religious myths—which include both doctrines and narratives—is a function of their rightly relating, or orienting, those who live by them to the noumenal Real.[1]

In principle, then, there is no difference between the proposition "God exists," the gospel narratives, through which Christians believe that they encounter the regenerating spirit of the God of Jesus Christ, the Upaniṣadic proclamation *sarvamhyetadbrahma*: "All this is certainly Brahman,"[2] and the multifarious narrations of the *līlā*, or the cosmic sport, of the gods and goddesses in the Hindu scriptures known as the Purāṇas.

Since any of these and other doctrinal proclamations and stories may, hypothetically, orient the hearer to the noumenal Real, they—given Hick's new definition of religious cognitivity—are to be accepted as cognitive. The test of their truth or falsity is not an eschatological test designed to mimic verificationist methods of confirming or disconfirming propositions, but whether they savingly orient their adherents to the noumenal Real. Thus, in addition to believing that knowledge comes through logic and the study of nature, Hick now holds that it also comes through metaphor, broadly conceived so as to include such extended metaphors as religious myths, whether presented in the form of narratives or doctrinal systems.

Hick and Religious Pluralism

Hick's interest in religious pluralism is not merely theoretical, but was motivated originally by his controversial ecclesiastical and political involvement in the sixties and seventies in an antiracist group in the English immigrant city of Birmingham that included Christians, Jews, Muslims, Hindus, Sikhs, Marxists, and humanists. As a member of a committee composed of members of the various religions represented in Birmingham, Hick helped to draw up a multifaith syllabus to replace the exclusively Christian religious instruction materials used in the Birmingham school system. Involvements such as these led Hick to reject the Christian exclusivism that he had adhered to unthinkingly since his adolescent conversion and to begin rethinking the relationship between the Christian and other religious traditions.[3]

These experiences and re-evaluations challenged Hick's conviction that religions are cognitive. Frequently the adherents of one religion make theological or metaphysical claims that are contrary to parallel claims made by adherents of other religions. There is, however, no commonly accepted procedure for deciding between these claims. As a datum of the phenomenology of religions, this diversity, in Hick's view, does not present a philosophical problem.[4] A philosophical issue arises when one considers that *each* of these contrary doctrinal and narrative traditions contends that it is a valid cognitive response to a divine reality. For example, Christians speak of the ultimacy of a personal God whose character is exhibited in stories that depict the acts and personality of Jesus, while Buddhists speak of the ultimacy of the truth of relativity, or interdependent origination, of all phenomena, as perceived and taught by the Buddha. These doctrines are contraries, since the Christian view is irreducibly personalistic, while the Buddhist view denies the ultimacy of personhood.[5] As Hick acknowledges: "surely these reported ultimates, personal and non-personal, are mutually exclusive" (IR, 234). That is, as contraries, both views can be false, but not more than one can be true.

The circumstance that the adherents of the views just mentioned and other contrary views *all* contend that their view is *the* true view easily lends itself to skepticism when one considers some of the implications of the logic of contraries.[6] Hick quotes a passage from David Hume's *Enquiries*, in which Hume's inquiry into miracles (rather than the differences in doctrine and experience with which Hick is concerned) led Hume to a wholesale religious skepticism. Hume writes:

> Let us consider, that, in matters, of religion, whatever is different is contrary; and that it is impossible the religions of ancient Rome, of Turkey, of Siam, and of China should, *all of them,* be established on any sound foundation. Every miracle, therefore, pretended to have been wrought in any of these religions (and all of them abound in miracles), as its direct scope is to establish the particular system to which it is attributed; so has it the force, though more indirectly, to overthrow every other system.[7]

The point somewhat obscurely expressed in this passage is that miracles cannot establish religion x at the expense of all others, since *all* religions (at least according to Hume) make use of miracles to establish themselves and discredit the others. Thus, all religions discredit all other religions, leaving none that are not overthrown. Out of its own many mouths, then, religion shows itself to be insupportable, an outcome justifying a wholesale religious skepticism and noncognitivism.

In support of this point, Hick also quotes the following statement from Bertrand Russell: "It is evident as a matter of logic that, since [the great religions of the world] disagree, not more than one of them can be true."[8] At first glance, this statement may seem to support religious particularism in the strong sense of exclusivism.[9] Actually, Russell certainly meant by this reasoning to show the illogicality of religious faith, since all religions claim to be true, though they teach contrary doctrines. For if the teachings of the different religions are contraries, then, in accordance with the logic of contraries, all religious doctrines could be false, but not more than *one* of them could be said to be true without falling into contradiction. Yet all religions claim their doctrines to be true, though these doctrines are contraries. Consequently, contradiction pervades the welter of plural visions of reality prescribed by the religious traditions of the world. This clamor of inconsistent voices, often speaking with absolute conviction, invites, though it does not necessitate, a skeptical outlook on the part of the religious outsider about *all* religious claims.

This is the dilemma that motivates John Hick to begin developing the pluralistic hypothesis. He proposes this hypothesis in order to discredit two kinds of interpretation of religions that pose the most serious threat to continued belief in the cognitivity of religions: 1) a wholesale rejection of the cognitivity of religions because of the inconsistent diversity of their ultimate claims; 2) a limitation of cognitivity to one particular religious tradition, a claim that when examined also leads to skepticism.[10] The first kind of interpretations Hick inaccurately calls *naturalistic*;[11] the second kind, he calls *confessional*[12] (I will replace these terms throughout with *noncognitive* and *particularist*).

As an alternative to these kinds of interpretation, Hick proposes "a religious interpretation of religion":

> There are many general interpretations of religion. These have usually been either naturalistic, treating religion as a purely human phenomenon, or, if religious, have been developed within the confines of a particular confessional conviction which construes all other traditions in its own terms. The one type of theory that has seldom been attempted is a *religious* but not confessional interpretation of religion in its plurality of

forms; and it is this that I shall be trying to offer [in *An Interpretation of Religion*] (*IR*, 1).

In the third type of theory, which aspires to be religious without being confessional, Hick tries to cut a middle course between particularism and noncognitivism (or confessionalism and naturalism). Hick hopes to avoid particularism by submitting to "the intellectual Golden Rule" that one ought to treat the religions of others as one would have one's own religion treated:

> Persons living within other traditions . . . are equally justified in trusting their own distinctive religious experience and in forming their beliefs on the basis of it. . . . let us avoid the implausibly arbitrary dogma that religious experience is all delusory with the single exception of the particular form enjoyed by the one who is speaking (*IR*, 235).[13]

Hick hopes to avoid skepticism and noncognitivism by pointing out that neither is a necessary implication of disagreement on ultimate issues between religions: "Is not belief in the divine, or the transcendent, undermined by this very variety? The question is an entirely proper one; and I believe that the correct answer is No" (*WBG*, 102).

Hick's confidence in so firmly answering this question in the negative derives from his holding to a view of religion, familiar from mystical writings, which has been developed in many religious traditions as a direct response to religious diversity. Upon this mystical view, Hick bases his religious interpretation of religion, which holds "that the great post-axial faiths constitute different ways of experiencing, conceiving and living in relation to an ultimate divine Reality which transcends all our varied visions of it" (*IR*, 36).

This mystical distinction between an ultimate divine Reality (however conceived) and the various religions signifying it is a familiar one to those who study religion. On this view, what is of most importance in determining the cognitivity of religions is not their specific doctrines and stories, but rather their common attempt, albeit in different idioms, to signify the different aspects of the supreme reality to which each points and to which each leads. However, this way of conceiving the relations of religions to the divine is not without difficulties.

Hick's Philosophy of Religions:
Perennialist or Constructivist?

Given his use of this mystical distinction, it may appear that Hick can be placed within that enduring though currently less fashionable school of philosophy of religions[14] known as *perennialism*, which has been expressed in varying ways by such diverse thinkers as Aldous Huxley, Sarvapelli Radhakrishnan, Frithjof Schuon, René Guénon, W. T. Stace, Huston Smith, Seyyed Hossein Nasr, and others. Perennialism is essentially the claim that all religions, despite their virtually infinite variety, share a common phenomenological structure that informs the *religious* experience of *all* religious people. This experience has a core of common characteristics: in mystical or religious experience one confronts a blissful and holy Reality, which infinitely transcends the varied realms of experience and language and which incessantly, though not deterministically, impels all beings ever to reach with more openness toward the never fully comprehensible or effable but finally saving truth of Reality itself. To cite just a few familiar names from the world's religious and philosophical tradition, this Ultimate Reality can be called God, the Absolute, the One, Truth, the Real, Brahman, Dharmākaya, the Tao, or al-Ḥaqq.

This familiar interpretation of religious diversity is reductionistic in one of two ways: either—as in the case of Stace—perennialism minimizes the rich doctrinal and narrative diversity of the religions by seeing it as an accidental product of history, society, and biography and which thus serves merely to decline the perennial truth in its different but dispensable dialects.[15] Or perennialism—as with Nasr, Schuon, and Guénon—retains a reverence for the diversity of religious traditions and insists that unless one is a pious and traditionalist participant in a distinctive religious tradition, one cannot understand religion or have true religious experience. However, despite this concern for distinctive traditions, this latter variety of perennialism still conceives these different traditions to be but different idioms of the unique intellectual apprehension of the One Ultimate Reality, which is the esoteric illumination vouchsafed to the gifted few who are able to penetrate the exoteric and diverse features of the different sacred traditions.[16]

Because Hick retains a lively sense of the effects of culture upon the construction of religious doctrine and stories it would be inaccurate simply to place him within the perennialist camp. Hick shares much in common with the constructivist philosophy of religions, inaugurated in the late seventies by Steven T. Katz and others and articulated in two significant volumes edited by Katz.[17]

Constructivism consciously departs from the reductionism of perennialism and pleads for "the recognition of differences" between the varieties of religious experience presented by the many religions of the world.[18] Constructivism, with Katz in the lead, has dominated the academic discussion of religious experience and mysticism for nearly two decades.[19] At its simplest, this new movement in the philosophy of religions claims, against all varieties of perennialism, that there are no unmediated experiences of a single mystical reality. Rather, because human beings are inescapably social and historical beings, there are different varieties of mysticism. There is a Hindu mysticism, a Jewish mysticism, a Buddhist mysticism, an Islāmic mysticism, and so on. Each of these is irreducibly different from the others and cannot be reduced to any of them, as in inclusivism, the more generous form of particularism, nor to some more basic, universal esoteric truth, as in perennialism.

In short, Katz and his fellow constructivists reject the exoteric/esoteric distinction, which is of such importance to the perennialists. Katz forcefully argues that it does serious violence to Buddhist mysticism and to Jewish mysticism, for instance, to assert that *devekuth*, the ultimate Jewish mystical experience, and *nirvāṇa*, the ultimate Buddhist mystical experience, are merely different *exoteric* ways of talking about the same *esoteric* experience.[20] Katz writes:

> Whatever *nirvāṇa* is, and indeed whatever *devekuth* is, in so far as words mean anything and philosophical inquiry has any significance, there is no way that one can describe, let alone equate, the experience of *nirvāṇa* and *devekuth* on the basis of the evidence. There is no intelligible way that anyone can legitimately argue that a 'no-self' experience of 'empty' calm is the same experience as the experience of intense loving, intimate relationship between two substantial selves, one of whom is conceived of as the personal God of western religion and all that this entails.[21]

Perhaps because of the prominence of the constructivist approach after the late seventies, Hick's attempt to formulate an interpretation of religions takes on a more self-consciously constructivist cast in his later writings on this topic.[22] Despite siding with the constructivists, Hick's continuing impulse to find some commonality among religions vitiates his allegiance to Katzian constructivism. Hick's apparent vacillation in his support of constructivism, despite his pledges of fealty to it, may most likely be traced back to his basic standpoint that the religions are culturally and irreducibly diverse significations of an ultimate divine reality, which transcends all of its significations, a position closer to perennialism than to constructivism. Writing a few years before the rise of constructivism, Hick expressed a perennialist intention in contemplating a global theology that "would consist in a body of hypotheses about the nature of reality, expressing the *basic common ground of the world religions*, and receiving mythic expression and devotional content in different ways within historical traditions" (*DEL*, 30 [emphasis mine]).

More recently Hick still evidenced a tendency toward perennialism. In *An Interpretation of Religion*, he declares that his interpretation of religions will primarily focus on belief in the transcendent as the common element in religions. He puts this essentialist definition to work immediately by using it to exclude Marxism as a form of religion (*IR*, 5–6)

Perhaps Hick vacillates because he wants to avoid the extremisms of constructivism (denial of a mystical 'common core'[23] of all religions), of religious noncognitivists (denial of the ontological realism of religious language in general), and of particularists (denial of the veridicality of religions other than one's own). Hick wants to develop a multidimensional view that will allow him to affirm the irreducible cultural differences, the ontological realism, the irreconcilable diversity, and the ineradicable cognitivity of religions. These not easily synthesizable intentions provide the tensions that have driven the evolution over the past two decades of Hick's understanding of religious pluralism.

Hick's Theology of Religions and
Early Philosophy of Religions

In attempting to work out an interpretation of religions that will slight neither their diversity nor their cognitivity,[24] Hick has passed through two phases. In the first, beginning around 1970, he proposed a Christian *theology* of religions,[25] one which has become quite influential and which still stands for many religious scholars as Hick's basic position.[26] However, in response to criticism of his theology of religions, Hick probed more deeply into the underlying issues of religious pluralism and began, around 1980, to develop a *philosophy* of religions,[27] an effort that culminated in his most complete statement on the subject, *An Interpretation of Religion: Human Responses to the Transcendent*, published in 1989.

Hick has moved in this direction over the past dozen years not merely in response to the sorts of criticism briefly recounted below, but because what was originally a theological issue for Hick has now become for him a fundamentally philosophical issue—an issue to which he brings not only the expertise of a major contemporary theologian (as evidenced by his writings in the area of theodicy, Christology, and thanatology) but also expertise as one of the world's leading philosophers of religion (as evidenced by his writings on the ontological argument, the nature of religious language, and the construction of religious experience).

Hick's Theology of Religions

In his earliest attempt to address the issue of religious pluralism, Hick wrote in 1970 that

> it is . . . possible to consider the hypothesis that the great religions are all, at their experiential roots, in contact with the same ultimate divine reality, but that their differing experiences of that reality, interacting over the centuries with the different thought forms of different cultures, have led to increasing differentiation and contrasting elaboration.[28]

Hick elaborated this view in a 1972 essay:

> Let us begin with the recognition, which is made in all the main religious traditions, that the ultimate divine reality is infinite and as such transcends the grasp of the human mind. . . . From this it follows that the different encounters with the transcendent within the different religious traditions may all be encounters with the one infinite reality, though with partially different and overlapping aspects of that reality (*GUF*, 139).

This distinction between a transcendent divine reality and the multitude of human responses to it continues to be a standard

feature of Hick's account of religion.[29] To bring out the usefulness
of this distinction, Hick frequently appeals to a set of more or less
familiar examples, such as the Hindu distinction between *nirguṇa*
Brahman (Brahman without attributes) and *saguṇa* Brahman
(Brahman with attributes); the Mahāyāna Buddhist distinction
between the ultimate, formless Dharmakāya (emptiness, suchness,
or the unmanifest and transcendent Buddha beyond all forms and
bodies) and its concretizations in the Saṃbhogakāya (bodies of
the Buddha seen in meditative visions) and the Nirmāṇakāya (the
human body of the historical Buddha);[30] the Pure Land Buddhist
distinction between *dharmatā dharmakāya,* or *nirvāṇa* as such,
and *upāya dharmakāya,* or *nirvāṇa* manifesting as Amida, the
Buddha of infinite compassion; the Sufi distinction between al-
Ḥaqq, the abyss of the Godhead, and Allāh, who is revealed out
of the abyss; Eckhart's distinction between the Godhead (*Gottheit*
or *deitas*) and God (*Gott* or *Deus*), and Gordon D. Kaufman's distinction between the "real God" and the "available God."[31] In
staking out this position, Hick is taking up a position as old as the
Ṛg Veda, where it is written that "the real is one, the learned call it
by many names, Agni, Yama, Mātariśvan";[32] as old also as the
fragment of Heracleitus in which it is written, "that which alone is
wise is one; it is willing and unwilling to be called by the name of
Zeus."[33] (Surprisingly, Hick has chosen not to elaborate this distinction in concepts close to hand and familiar to most Western
theologians, i.e., cataphatic theology and apophatic theology, or
positive and negative theology.[34] These concepts may be taken as
fulfilling the same purpose in Christian theologies as the *saguṇa/
nirguṇa* Brahman distinction in Hindu theologies.[35]) This essentially mystical distinction is at the center of Hick's controversial
and influential writings in the early seventies in the Christian theology of religions in which he called for "a Copernican revolution
in theology."

The Copernican revolution in theology. In "The Copernican Revolution in Theology" (1972),[36] Hick eloquently and concisely issued the call for what was then—and for some theologians still is—a radical shift in Christian thinking: a revolution in Christian theology in which the religions of the world would no longer be made to revolve around Christianity but in which all of the religions would be allowed to revolve around God. Hick proposed this new departure in Christian thinking by analogy to the revolution in astronomy initiated by Copernicus when he proposed a new and more elegant heliocentric cosmological model to replace the ornate epicyclic and geocentric model of Ptolemy.

Hick's proposal went far beyond even the most radically inclusivistic theologies issuing out of Vatican II, such as Karl Rahner's notion of pious non-Christians as "anonymous Christians," and the younger Hans Küng's distinction between religions other than Christianity as ordinary ways of salvation and Catholic Christianity as the extraordinary way of salvation. As generous as these theories attempted to be, Hick saw them as nothing more than elegant epicycles designed to preserve the particularistic, Christocentric view of the religious life of humanity, in which all that is good in human religion is seen as finding its fulfillment in the Christian faith. These theories were certainly a decided improvement upon the ancient Roman Catholic exclusivistic doctrine *extra ecclesiam nulla salus*: "outside the church there is no salvation" (or in its Protestant version: outside Christ there is no salvation). Hick, however, took a radically different position when he called for a Copernican revolution in theology in which Christians would abandon as futile and imperialistic all attempts at saving what in this age of rapidly increasing interreligious contacts is the now untenable belief that Christianity—or for that matter, any religion—is the center around which the other religions revolve. In the new age of religious ecumenism that is now dawning, God, in Hick's view, ought to be the center around which the religions revolve (*PRP*, 51–53).

Objections to the Copernican revolution in theology. Theological criticism of Hick's Copernican revolution has centered upon the meaning that *God* has in a post-Ptolemaic theology of religions. If by *God* Hick retains some notion of the personal God revealed in the Christian scriptures (or of some other revelatory tradition, such as Islām or theistic Hinduism), then he has regressed to the Ptolemaic standpoint and is covertly working with a *Christian* (or *Muslim* or *Hindu*) theistic conception as the criterion for evaluating what will count as the meaning of *God*.[37] If on the other hand, he uses *God* in such a way that it has no relation to any of the received notions of God in the world's religious traditions, then his position results in what Gavin D'Costa calls "transcendental agnosticism"[38] or, according to Duncan B. Forrester, in a "relativism which is unlikely to be acceptable to committed believers except for Vedantic Hindus."[39] Thus, as Julius Lipner writes: "the understanding of God . . . reached will either be too broad to give any impetus to inter-religious dialogue, or too narrow for a Copernican perspective."[40]

Another difficulty with the use of *God* in Hick's Copernican theology of religions is that it excludes nontheistic religions, such as many schools of Buddhism and Hinduism (unless *God* be interpreted so broadly as to exclude from it any reference to personal attributes). It also excludes from religious consideration, the secular ideology of Marxism, which, Forrester claims, shares more concerns with Christianity than with nontheistic Hinduism.[41]

Hick's First Attempts at a Philosophy of Religions

Hick began to respond to these criticisms in 1980 with the publication of the article "Toward a Philosophy of Religious Pluralism,"[42] in which he first turns his attention to working out in detail, along quasi-Kantian lines, a *philosophy* as opposed to a *theology* of religions. In this article, Hick unhesitatingly accepts the criticisms of his use of the term *God* and attempts to clarify matters. He acknowledges that such terms as *the Transcendent, the Absolute, the Tao, Brahman,* and so forth, while possibly less limiting than *God,* with its theistic implications, are not "fully tradition-neutral or tradition-transcending" terms for the postulated transcendent reality and that, therefore, if one wants to refer in any way to the transcendent divine reality, one is "obliged to use a term provided by a particular tradition." Consequently, he writes that

> as a Christian I shall accordingly use the word "God," but I shall not use it in a straightforwardly theistic sense. There is of course the danger that either the writer or the reader may slip back, without noticing it, into the standard [theistic] use of the term; and both must be vigilant against this. I shall . . . speak of God, but with the important proviso that it is an open question at this stage whether, and if so in what sense, God is personal. . . . God is neither a person or a thing, but is the transcendent reality which is conceived and experienced by different human mentalities in both personal and impersonal ways (*GHMNUS,* 91).

Within a few years, however, Hick abandoned even this qualified use of the term *God.* In a later article (1984), in which he renewed his call for a Copernican revolution, Hick now wants to trade in the old Christianity-centered universe not for a *theocentric* universe of faiths but for a *Reality-centered* universe, which "centres upon the divine Reality; and Christianity is seen as one of a number of worlds of faith which circle around and reflect that Reality" (*PRP,* 53).

Hick offers no explanation for this shift in terminology, although it seems obvious that it is meant to outmaneuver those, like Lipner and D'Costa, who have criticized his use of *God* as either too narrow or too broad a term to be at the center of the religious universe. In *An Interpretation of Religion*, Hick calls this divine Reality "the Real" and he offers what he thinks are good reasons why this term, though it certainly derives from the traditions of the West and from the Latin tongue, is an acceptable replacement for *God*.[43] However, such a change of terminology is not likely to convince those who criticized his theocentric standpoint. Anticipating Hick's move beyond the term *God*, Lipner, in an article published in 1977, asserted that a move such as this would be *too easy* and would not get at the fundamental problem with the Copernican revolution—that of determining the nature of the postulated center of the universe of faiths: "Nor will it do, of course, to insist that it is not intended to stress any *concept* of 'God' or 'The Absolute' or whatever in this reconstructed theology. For all the old objections crop us again."[44]

These old objections are the ones mentioned above. As with *God*, so it is for *the Absolute* or *the Real:* either the understanding of these terms will be too broad (indeterminate with respect to theistic and nontheistic conceptions) or too narrow (asserting a specific theistic or nontheistic conception).

To these objections Hick proposes an answer in his *fully developed* philosophy of religions. He tries to bypass these criticisms of the use of the term *the Real* by arguing that the Real *an sich*, or the noumenal Real, transcends all modes of language, whether negative or positive, and so cannot be conceived as either *saguna* (with attributes) or *nirguna* (without attributes). That is, the noumenal Real, as conceived by Hick, utterly transcends the categories of personal God or impersonal Absolute. In Hick's latest conception of the divine reality, it utterly transcends all the traditional distinctions, mentioned above, between a manifest and unmanifest divine reality. The noumenal Real is neither *Gott* nor *Gottheit*, neither *saguṇa* Brahman nor *nirguṇa* Brahman, neither Allāh nor al-Ḥaqq, neither the "available God" nor the "real God."

The Pluralistic Hypothesis and Kant's First Critique

In developing his philosophy of religions over the last decade, Hick began subordinating the mystical distinction described above to the philosophical distinction between noumena and phenomena, which he derives from Kant's First Critique.[45] No longer writing simply as a Christian theologian wanting to understand the place of Christianity in the universe of faiths, Hick now writes as a philosopher who wants to understand the general relations between religions and their postulated ground. Thus, Hick suggests that the religions are best understood "as different phenomenal experiences of the one divine noumenon" (*GHMNUS*, 94)

This wresting of Kant's noumena/phenomena distinction out of its proper context in the analysis of the perception of objects of sense and making it serve as an explanation for the different visions of the various religious traditions is the philosophical basis of the pluralistic hypothesis. Hick works out this philosophical hypothesis with a conceptuality alien to religion that was introduced by Kant in the First Critique. (Since Hick puts this conceptuality to a purpose fundamentally at odds with Kant's own use of this conceptuality, I call this hypothesis quasi-Kantian.) Along with the notions of noumena and phenomena, Hick also presses into service the Kantian conceptions of experience-constituting categories and the temporal schematization of these categories. With the aid of these conceptions, Hick proposes develop an epistemology of religion that will account both for the cognitivity and the diversity of religious claims and worldviews, thereby avoiding both skepticism (along with its theological modification, religious noncognitivism) and particularism.

The noumenon/phenomenon distinction. The distinction between the Real *an sich* and the Real as phenomenally expressed in the different religious traditions is the most basic notion of Hick's pluralistic hypothesis. Hick describes this as

> the distinction . . . between something as it is in itself and as it appears to a consciousness dependent upon a particular kind of perceptual machinery and endowed with a particular system of interpretive concepts congealed into a linguistic system (*IR*, 14; see also 236).

As is immediately evident this distinction is inspired by Kant's distinction between phenomena and noumena. Kant distinguishes these two terms as follows:

> If we entitle certain objects, as appearances, sensible entities (phenomena), then since we thus distinguish the mode in which we intuit them from the nature that belongs to them in themselves, it is implied in this distinction that we place the latter, considered in their own nature, although we do not so intuit them, or that we place other possible things, which are not objects of our senses but are thought as objects merely through the understanding, in opposition to the former, and that in so doing we entitle them intelligible entities (noumena).[46]

Or, more simply, "by 'noumenon' we mean a thing so far as it is *not an object of our sensible intuition,* and so abstract from our mode of intuiting it."[47]

Taking his lead from Kant, Hick argues that the human senses and the mind/brain are affected by an environing reality that can never be known, experienced, or described in itself:

> Thus although we cannot speak of the Real *an sich* in literal terms, nevertheless we live inescapably in relation to it, and in all that we do and undergo we are having to do with it as well as, and in terms of, our more proximate situations (*IR*, 351; see also 134, 136).[48]

This environing reality Hick calls the *Real* an sich (or the noumenal Real) and the various ways that this noumenal reality is produced in human experience he calls phenomena.[49] Hick summarizes his interpretation of the quasi-Kantian analysis of how the phenomenal world of sense perception is constructed by the mind: "informational input from external reality [is] interpreted by the mind in terms of its own categorial scheme and thus [comes] to consciousness as meaningful phenomenal experience" (*IR*, 243).[50]

Hick sees this as analogous to the transformation of the noumenal Real is transformed into the diverse religious phenomena (*IR*, 243). He claims that "as in the case of our awareness of the physical world, the environing divine reality is brought to consciousness in terms of certain basic concepts or categories" (*IR*, 245).

Hick radically differs from Kant in that Hick uses the noumenon/phenomenon distinction not only in the analysis of sensory experience but also of religious experience (or, in Hick's language, religious awareness of the Real [*IR*, 243–4]), a use of the distinction that Kant would not have allowed (*IR*, 240, 242–243).[51] Aware that this application of Kant's critical philosophy to religion will strike many as illegitimate, Hick argues that

> Kant was solely concerned, in his discussion of the categories, with the construction of the physical world in sense perception. One who is concerned with the construction of the divine within religious experience has the option of accepting or rejecting Kant's view of sense perception. One theory neither requires nor is incompatible with the other. We have already noted that Kant's own epistemology of religion was quite unrelated to his understanding of sense perception. But this fact does not bar others, inspired by his basic insights, from seeing religious and sense experience as continuous in kind, thereby extending Kant's analysis of the one, in an appropriately adapted form, to the other (*IR*, 24).

Kant's First Critique is difficult to interpret, since it contains a number of lines of argument whose mutual coherence is open to question (*IR*, 240).[52] Of these lines of argument, Hick deliberately chooses that strand of Kant's thought in the First Critique in which Kant *apparently* maintained a fundamental distinction between an actual, independent, and uninterpreted reality and its schematizations in experience.[53] Hick writes:

> In this strand of Kant's thought—not the only strand, but the one I am seeking to press into service in the epistemology of religion—the noumenal world exists independently of our perception of it and the phenomenal world is that same world as it appears to our human consciousness (*IR*, 241).[54]

By attempting to subordinate the construction of religious experience to the same constraints as those imposed by Kant upon sensible intuition, Hick implies that religious experience has to do *only* with religious phenomena, such as the humanly constructed concepts of the noumenal Real like Allāh, Yahweh, Kr̥ṣṇa, Brahman, Dharmakāya, and so forth and never with the noumenal Real—*never with the ultimate religious reality itself.*[55] Hick claims (in an essay written before he had hit upon using the term *the Real*) "that religious experience is experience of the Transcendent [i.e., the noumenal Real], not however, as divine noumenon but as divine phenomenon."[56]

This is an even more radical position than Kant's, since Kant doesn't deny the *possibility* that there may be intellectual intuition of noumena, but only that human beings do not *in actuality* possess the faculty of intellectual intuition.[57] As Kant points out in the first edition of the First Critique, if intellectual intuition were possible for human beings, then

> a field quite different from that of the senses would here lie open to us, a world which is thought as it were in the spirit (or even perhaps intuited), and which would therefore be for the understanding a far nobler, not a less noble, object of contemplation.[58]

This is not much of a concession by Kant to the notion of intellectual intuition, since Kant holds that the reality intended by the concept "noumenon" is unknowable because human beings possess *only* sensible intuition,[59] which implies the rejection of any sort of religious experience that relies upon intellectual intuition of objects beyond the range of the senses. On this point, however, Hick betrays no ambiguity and cuts off all appeals to a special faculty of knowing the noumenal Real as it is in itself, declaring, "that even in the profoundest unitive mysticism the mind operates with culturally specific concepts and that what is experienced is accordingly a manifestation of the Real rather than the Real *an sich*" (IR, 295).

Thus we confront a disturbing paradox in Hick's hypothesis: *He holds that we can be aware of, meditate upon, and worship the noumenal Real, even though we can never know it or experience it* (IR, 243, 350–351).

Hick tries to avoid this paradox by offering an *ad hoc* analysis of the relationship between the noumenal Real and human religious experience. As indicated in the following diagram, he conceives this relationship as a threefold scale of steps between the transcendent reality as it exists in itself and actual human religious experience:

The Noumenal Divine Real	»	Independent of Religious Experience
Categories: God, the Absolute	»	General Structure of Religious Experience
Schematizations: (Im)Personae	»	Religious Experience in the Traditions[60]

As indicated in this diagram, the two categories, God and the Absolute, mediate between the one noumenal Real, on the one side, and the various culturally schematized *personae* (or personal expressions of the Real) and *impersonae* (or impersonal expressions of the Real) of the world's religious traditions, on the other

(*IR*, 244–45). Since the impersonae and the personae are phenomenal schematizations of the noumenal Real, neither apply directly to that reality, although both classes are soteriologically and experientially aligned with the one ineffable, noumenal Real.[61] Thus, in Hick's view, as indicated by this diagram, awareness of the impact, or "presence," of the noumenal Real is always mediated by one or the other of these categories.[62]

The relationships suggested by this diagram are dubious, however, since they do not actually show how an unknowable Real becomes knowable; on the contrary, this diagram attempts to disguise the problem behind the facade of an illusory solution. The relationship between the first step of the diagram, the noumenal Real, which Hick thinks is independent of religious experience, and the second step, the categories, which he takes as the basic structure of religious experience, is obscure. The diagram offers no clue to the resolution of the remaining mystery: how is the inconceivable transformed into conceptions? There is here only an appearance of an answer to this difficult question.

Categories. Although Hick agrees with Kant on the function of the categories in the synthesis of possible experiences, Hick radically departs from Kant in expanding the range of possible experience by introducing two categories that would have been rejected outright by Kant: the categories of God and the Absolute. Not only would Kant have rejected these categories because they extend "further than experience can follow,"[63] he would also have rejected them because his own categories are universal and necessary, while Hick's are neither, but are, as Hick admits, "culture-relative" (*IR*, 244).

God and *the Absolute* have novel technical meanings in Hick's usage: *God* signifies theistic varieties of religious experience in which human beings relate themselves as persons to personal deities, while *the Absolute* signifies nondualistic varieties of religious experience in which human beings attempt to submerge their individual personalities in an impersonal or transpersonal reality (*IR*, 243–245). Hick models these religious categories on Kant's twelve categories of the understanding, which, in Kant's view, are the "first seeds and dispositions in the human understanding"[64] and which produce experience when stimulated by the senses. As Kant writes: "the impressions of sense supplying the first stimulus, the whole faculty of knowledge opens out to them, and experience is brought into existence."[65]

Hick conceives his two categories as functioning in exactly the same way as Kant's categories (so long as Kant is interpreted as a "problematic realist"[66]). For Hick (who may also be interpreted as a problematic realist) the noumenal Real is an *independent reality* that the mind transforms into the phenomena of religious experience by schematizing the categories of God and the Absolute (*IR*, 243).

There is no place in Kant's categorial scheme for the categories God and the Absolute, since Kant, unlike Hick, did not see religion as grounded in a kind of intuition[67] that includes not merely constructive encounters with the noumena of sense but also with the noumenon of the spirit. Hick's view on this point, however, is, as I will argue in the next chapter, incoherent, involving as it does the supposed intuition of a noumenal reality that is itself unknowable and nonintuitable.

Schematization: (im)personae. Borrowing another concept from the First Critique, Hick claims that the two basic categories, God and the Absolute, are schematized, or concretized, within actual religious experience as the variety of gods and absolutes worshipped in the religious traditions. These concretizations Hick calls the *personae* and the *impersonae* of the noumenal Real (*IR*,

245). Just as time schematizes, or concretizes, the Kantian categories of the understanding (e.g., "the pure concept of substance is schematized as the more concrete object of an idea enduring through time"[*IR*, 243]), so in Hick's view, the range of diverse human cultures schematizes or concretizes the categories of God and the Absolute.[68]

Thus, in Hick's view, the noumenal Real may be related to through either category (the implied element of human choice here undercuts the Kantian notion of a category, which is universal and necessary and thus precludes choosing among them); it will be schematized accordingly, personally or impersonally. Kṛṣṇa, Allāh, Baldur, the God of Israel, and so forth schematize awareness of the noumenal Real through the category of God, while Brahman, Dharmakāya, Tao, and so forth schematize awareness of the noumenal Real through the category of the Absolute.

In this way Hick tries to support the paradoxical claim that the inexperienceable and unknowable Real *an sich* is nevertheless the object of the varieties of religious experience found in the religions of the world. He writes, "we . . . only experience the Real as its presence affects our distinctively human modes of consciousness" (*IR*, 173). The varied content of the diverse phenomenal schematizations of the Real, and not the noumenal Real itself, provides the content of the varieties of human religious experience. Thus, the noumenal Real is merely the *formal occasion but not the substantive cause* of the varieties of religious experience (*IR*, 243; see also 350–51). As Hick writes:

> The divine Reality is not directly known *an sich*. But when human beings relate themselves to it in the mode of an I–Thou encounter they experience it as personal. . . . When human beings relate themselves to the Real in the mode of non-personal awareness they experience it as non-personal (*IR*, 245).

That is, Hick claims that the noumenal Real is *neutral* with respect to the various *personae* and *impersonae* that human beings construct to schematize it. Nothing of the noumenal Real except the simple fact of its implied existence enters into the construction of these phenomenal images of the divine reality.[69] Apart from the unverifiable claim that the noumenal Real exists, Hick's view of religion would immediately collapse into a noncognitivist functionalism or phenomenology.

Hick's Turn to Mythological Truth

Given this highly attenuated relationship between the noumenal Real and its phenomenal images, what path, if any, remains open for meaningful religious language? Here Hick turns the notion of myth to his purposes. He writes that the

> relationship between the ultimate noumenon and its multiple phenomenal appearances, or between the limitless, transcendent reality and our many partial human images of it makes possible mythological speech about the Real. I define a myth as a story or statement which is not literally true but which tends to evoke an appropriate *dispositional* attitude to its subject-matter. Thus the truth of a myth is a practical truthfulness: a true myth is one which *rightly relates us* to a reality about which we cannot speak in non-mythological terms (*IR*, 247–248).[70]

Here we see an interesting turnabout in Hick's thought. From his insistence in earlier writings on the fact-asserting character of particular religious doctrines, Hick, under the impulse of religious pluralism moves—right before our eyes in the pages of *An Interpretation of Religion*—in the direction of a pragmatic criterion of religious cognitivity: the soteriological orientation of schematization of the noumenal Real. This principle of cognitivity is not concerned with the truth-values of specific truth-claims but only with the judgment whether a particular doctrine, regardless of specific content, orients the religious practitioner to the unknowable, inexperienceable noumenal Real.

This position contrasts sharply with the view maintained in earlier years by Hick. In 1973, he claimed that "religion is concerned with reality and its central affirmations are, ultimately, true or false factual assertions."[71] This earlier view of factuality, or cognitivity, was directed toward particular religious doctrines. Thus, Hick noted that "it . . . remains a question of prime importance whether such sentences as 'God loves mankind' belong to the class of sentences that are either true or false."[72]

The Soteriological Criterion

Inevitably the question arises of how one can be justified in holding that religious phenomena—the various inconsistent doctrines and stories, or myths, of the religions—schematize an unknowable and inexperienceable x called *the noumenal Real?* How can one know the unknowable? Along with the metaphysical scheme outlined above, Hick also attempts to answer this question by resorting to what he calls *the soteriological criterion* (*IR*, 299), or the judgment that religious myths or doctrines are true

in so far as the dispositional responses which they tend to evoke are appropriate to our actual present situation as beings on the way towards salvation/liberation. If we have been right in seeing this goal as the transformation of human existence from self-centredness to Reality-centredness, eschatological myths are valid to the extent that they promote that transformation (*IR*, 355).

This outlook is consistent with the transcendental agnosticism, or what Hick calls a "doctrine of religious ignorance" (*IR*, 343), that is implicit in the pluralistic hypothesis, since Hick claims that

the truthfulness or untruthfulness of mythological stories, images, and conceptions does not consist in their literal adequacy to the nature of the Real *an sich*—in this respect it is not so much that they miss their target as that the target is totally beyond their range—but in their capacity to evoke appropriate or inappropriate dispositional responses to the Real (*IR*, 353).[73]

Hick claims no novelty for this view, in which the deliverances of theoretical reason are subordinated to criteria emanating from practical reason. He sees himself in agreement on this with Socrates and the mythic pictures that he embroidered in the Phaedo to liberate his disciples,[74] and with the Buddha's rejecting of serious concern with *diṭṭhi* ("speculative theories") and *avyakāta* ("unanswerable questions")[75] and focusing present religious concern upon what is conducive to the overcoming of the egoic construction of reality. This outlook is also consistent with Kant's rejection of speculative metaphysics and his grounding of the ethical and religious life in the requirements of practical reason (a position that is incompatible with the attempt to ground the veracity of religion in the Hickian metaphysical scheme outlined above). One is reminded of the story told by the Buddha about the foolishness of a person shot with a poisoned arrow who wants to know by whom he was shot and with what sort of arrow before letting the arrow be removed (*IR, 344*). Thus, the criterion of religious truth, or cognitivity, is no longer for Hick the possibility of experiential or eschatological verification of certain religious propositions, but rather the pragmatic soteriological criterion. Using this criterion one may ask whether a particular portrait or mythical expression of the noumenal Real aids or hinders what Christians call "salvation," what Hindus and Buddhists call "liberation," and what Hick calls "the realization of a limitlessly better possibility for human existence" (*IR, 374*).[76]

Since the myths of all religions have the same function—the realization of better human possibilities—there can be no real argument between them or need to make absolute choices between them. Hick claims that the mythic pictures provided by the religions

are true in so far as the responses which they tend to elicit are in soteriological alignment with the Real. Their truthfulness is the practical truthfulness which consists in guiding us aright. They therefore do not conflict with one another as would rival factual hypotheses. Different mythologies may each be valid as ways of evoking, within the life of a particular faith community, human self-transcendence in relation to the Real (*IR*, 375).

However, the claim that the widely divergent myths of the different traditions do not conflict with one another is a trivialization of the actual differences between myths. Hick's strategy for overcoming the doctrinal differences between religious traditions is to convert the inconsistent doctrines of the different religions into myths and then to claim that these myths only trivially differ from one another in their schematizations of the noumenal Real, though they all agree on the need to transcend the ego. This move neatly dispenses altogether with the controversial work of evaluating the specific truth-claims expressed by the often contrary doctrines of the religious traditions. Thus, all (post-axial) religions, despite their marked differences in basic teachings are more or less valid, according to the pluralistic hypothesis, not for any intrinsic reason connected with what they specifically teach but because they all evoke human self-transcendence in relation to the Real.[77]

Against the charge that this is a relativistic outcome and not merely reductionistic, one can defend Hick by pointing out that the pragmatic soteriological criterion by which he judges the worth of any religious myth is a *moral* criterion: the overcoming of self-regard in the direction of selfless service to others and the Real. This criterion is consistent with the highest virtues of saintliness as depicted in many religions, but inconsistent with religious myths that foster egoism, nationalism, tribalism, genocide, and other failings of religions. Thus, despite the reductionism fostered by the soteriological criterion, it is not a relativistic criterion.

It goes without saying that this approach is not likely to be congenial to those whose doctrines have first been called myths and then reduced in meaning to a rather thin soteriological claim about human self-transcendence. Consequently, Hick's pluralistic hypothesis has met with more criticism than acceptance. To a more detailed critique of the hypothesis, we will now turn our attention.

Notes

[1] Hick writes: "I define a myth as a story or statement which is not literally true but which tends to evoke an appropriate dispositional attitude to its subject-matter. Thus the truth of a myth is a practical truthfulness: a true myth is one which rightly relates us to a reality about which we cannot speak in non-mythological terms" (*IR*, 248). In his latest writings, Hick views myths, stories, and propositions as all potentially cognitive. In earlier writings Hick subordinated myth to culture and granted cognitive status only to propositions (*DEL*, 29). By *orient*, Hick means "rightly relating" (*IR*, 356), or disposing human beings (247) toward the noumenal Real.

[2] *Māṇḍūkyopaniṣad* 2 (trans. Nikhilānanda).

[3] See *GUF*, 121–122; "Three Controversies," in *PRP*, 6–10; *GHMNUS*, 16–18; Gavin D'Costa, *John Hick's Theology of Religions: A Critical Evaluation* (Lanham, MD: University Press of America, 1987), 12–16.

[4] As Hick writes: "From the point of view of phenomenology, or description, the fact of religious pluralism presents no philosophical problem. It just is the case that there are many different traditions of religious life and thought" (*GHMNUS*, 88).

[5] Any attempt to synthesize or mediate contrary religious doctrines, such as the theistic dualism of classical Christianity or theistic Hinduism with the nontheistic nondualism of Advaita Vedānta or Buddhism, will result in a doctrine that subordinates one of the contrary doctrines to the other, even if this subordination is irenically papered over for the sake of dialogue or "mutual understanding." Theists are not anonymous nondualists any more than nondualists are anonymous theists.

[6] Elsewhere Hick refers to the alternative visions of religious traditions as "mutually contradictory" (*IR*, 228). But Hick's use of *contradictory* is incorrect. He ought to have used *contrary*. In colloquial usage *contradictory* and *contrary* are often used synonymously. In logic, however, contradictory statements are so related that one *must* be false and the other *must* be true. Contrary statements, on the other hand, are so related that *all* of them may be false, while only *one* of them may be true. Thus, the Christian view that ultimate reality is a person and the Buddhist view that the interrelatedness of phenomena is the ultimately real are contraries,

since both could be false—it may be the case that Brahman, which, according to Advaita Vedānta, transcends both personhood and relationality, is true. Of course, each of these alternatives may be false and some other, as yet unmentioned alternative may be true. For example, atheistic humanism in alliance with materialistic monism may be the case.

[7] Quoted in *IR*, 229 (emphasis mine).

[8] Quoted in *IR*, 229.

[9] I use the term *particularist* to refer to two strategies taken by religious thinkers who hold that their tradition contains the final criteria of religious truth. The first of these two strategies is commonly called *exclusivism*, which is the belief that only the teachings of religion *x* are true, while those of other religions are categorically false. No dialogue or search for points of commonality with other religions is countenanced on this view. I call this position *strong particularism*. The second strategy is commonly called *inclusivism*, which is the belief that hints and foreshadowings of the ultimate truth of the true religion, *x*, may be found in other religions. This position encourages dialogue and a search for points of commonality. I call this position *weak particularism*. Both kinds of particularist believe that the ultimate criteria of religious truth are to be found only in the religion that she or he advocates.

[10] See *PRP*, 106; *WBG*, 102, 109; *IR*, 224, 228, 236, 249. One of the more ingenious religious responses to the skeptical challenges posed by the varieties of analytic philosophy in this century has been the development of views of religious language that discount its cognitivity and ontological pretensions but that still see religious language as serving important roles in human life, such as providing identity-forming and identity-preserving communities. This religious noncognitivism is the *religious* concession to religious skepticism that seeks to preserve various *uses* of religious language, despite the putative noncognitivity of such language.

[11] See Hick, *IR*, 1, 3, 111–118. Hick uses *naturalism* to mean interpretations of religion that view religion ultimately as a solely human creation devised to fulfill human needs (see especially 111). Hick includes many varieties of interpretation of religion under the rubric *naturalism*. These include such nonreligious interpretations of religion as those of Feuerbach, Marx, and Freud, which see religion as projection (111–115, 190–192), the view of religion as the construction of noncognitive symbolic contexts of human meaning, as in the work of Durkheim (115), John Herman Randall (196–198), and Clifford Geertz (196) on the nonreligious side, and Tillich on the religious side (196); the religious but noncognitivist interpretations of R. B. Braithwaite (193–195) and of the neo-Wittgensteinians Don Cupitt and D. Z. Phillips, which involve the rejection of the cognitivist, or realist, intention of religion while still cultivating religious forms of life as valuable in

their own right as expressions of *human* spirituality (198–201). What all of these varieties of interpretation of religion have in common is the rejection as essential to religious language of the realist intention that internally animates almost all forms of religion (excepting perhaps some interpretations of Buddhism [see 187]). On these interpretations, religious language is nonrealist and noncognitive. However, the inadequacy of Hick's use of *naturalism* as a class term for all of these varieties of interpretation is shown in his failure to recognize that there is a *cognitivist* religious naturalism, which sees religion as making in its own way cognitive claims that are consistent with nonreligious natural and social science, as in the cases of Henry Nelson Wieman (see his discussion of the *real* meaning of *God* in *Man's Ultimate Commitment* [Carbondale, IL: Southern Illinois University Press, 1958], 11–12) and John Dewey (he attempts a similar naturalistic recasting of God-talk in *A Common Faith* [New Haven: Yale University Press, 1934], 32–33). Since Hick uses *naturalistic, noncognitive, nonrealist*, and *skeptical* more or less synonymously, I think it best to substitute *nonrealist* or *noncognitive* for *naturalistic* when expounding Hick's critique of interpretations of religions that do not take seriously the idea that religions make claims about a reality not reducible to the creative activity of the tradition itself. I will also occasionally use the term *functionalist* to indicate these kinds of interpretations, a term not used by Hick, although it can be used as a synonym for *noncognitive* and *nonrealist*.

[12] See *IR*, 1, 235.

[13] See also *PRP*, 50.

[14] The use of the unfamiliar phrase *philosophy of religions* is intentional. The final *s* in this phrase serves the purpose of distinguishing what Hick is doing in his latest writings from the traditional philosophical topic known as philosophy of religion, which has traditionally been concerned with the basic questions of philosophical theism about the existence and nature of God and related questions and aporias. Without losing sight of this topic, Hick attempts in his philosophy of religions to develop a more comprehensive approach that is concerned with accounting for the relationship between a postulated divine reality and the various religious traditions of the world. The central question of this philosophical topic is: Why is the divine reality—the Real in Hick's terminology—productive of so many divergent and often exclusive religious traditions? Or, put in a more ontologically neutral way: Why are the different conceptions of the ultimate produced by the religious traditions of the world persistently taken by many thinkers to refer to the same ultimate reality? (Gavin D'Costa has also suggested the phrase *philosophy of religions* as more appropriate to the later, philosophical development of Hick's pluralistic theology of religions [*John Hick's Theology of Religions*, xi, n. 4]). Philosophy of religions must also be distinguished from Hick's views in theology of religions, which is a theological topic concerned with determining what consequences for *Christian* theology, doctrine, practice, and self-understanding

result from serious encounters with other living religious traditions.

[15] W. T. Stace, the late Princeton philosopher, was not concerned with the preservation of religious tradition but only with delineating what were the most basic elements, or the 'common core', of the various mystical traditions. Among these elements, Stace included the consciousness of the One, a sense of beatitude, a sense of the holy or the divine, a predilection for paradoxicality, and the claim that mystical experiences are ineffable (*Mysticism and Philosophy* [1960; reprint, Los Angeles: Jeremy P. Tarcher, Inc., 1987], 131–133). Steven T. Katz criticizes this approach as "too reductive and inflexible, forcing multifarious and extremely variegated forms of mystical experience into improper interpretive categories which lose sight of the fundamentally important differences between the data [of the different religions] studied," ("Language, Epistemology, and Mysticism," in *Mysticism and Philosophical Analysis*, ed. Steven T. Katz [New York: Oxford University Press, 1978], 25).

[16] Seyyed Hossein Nasr, *Knowledge and the Sacred* (1981; reprint, Albany: State University Press of New York, 1989), 75–81; Frithjof Schuon, *The Transcendent Unity of Religions* (Wheaton, IL: The Theosophical Publishing House, 1984), xxxiii–xxxiv. Among the numerous excellent works of perennialist writers, one of the most pleasurable to read is Nasr's 1981 Gifford Lectures, *Knowledge and the Sacred*. As with the writings of some of the other perennialists, such as Schuon and Guénon, Nasr's belief in the ultimate unity of the traditions in an intellectual apprehension of the Absolute Reality does not preclude a total immersion in authoritative religious traditions. In fact, this traditional view of knowledge demands that one immerse oneself fully in a way of being that is at odds with the putatively debilitating scientism, historicism, antitraditionalism, and liberalism of modernist cultures.

[17] *Mysticism and Philosophical Analysis* (1978) and *Mysticism and Religious Traditions* (New York: Oxford University Press, 1983). Hick claims in *DEL* (1976) that "the mythic and cultic substances of a religion are aspects of a civilization" (29), a view that partially anticipates Katz's volume on constructivism by two years. Concerning this issue, Hick wrote that "there has been considerable discussion in recent writings on philosophy of religion about whether, as W. T. Stace, Ninian Smart, and others have argued, 'phenomenologically, mysticism is everywhere the same' but is differently interpreted within the different religions, or whether, as Steven Katz, and others have argued, 'the experience itself as well as the form in which it is reported is shaped by concepts which the mystic brings to, and which shape, his experience.' In this debate I side with Katz" (*IR* 170–171 n. 17; see also 295–296, nn. 7, 8).

[18] Katz, *Mysticism and Philosophical Analysis*, 25.

[19] Among nonacademics the perennialist view remains the unchallenged paradigm

for understanding mystical experience. This is the case, for instance in harmonial, nonmainstream American religious movements, which include the older New Thought movements such as Unity, Religious Science, and Christian Science and the more recent New Age movements such as neo-Asian religions, neoshamanism, rebirthing, and groups studying channeled materials such as *A Course in Miracles* and *The Starseed Transmissions*. (On the meaning of the term *harmonial religion* as applied to the study of American religion, see Sidney E. Ahlstrom, *A Religious History of the American People* [New Haven: Yale University Press, 1972], where he describes harmonial religion as a particularly American religious movement, increasing in appeal since the nineteenth century, "in which spiritual composure, physical health, and even economic well-being are understood to flow from a person's rapport with the cosmos. Human beatitude and immortality are believed to depend to a great degree on one's being 'in tune with the infinite'" [1019]).

[20] Katz, *Mysticism and Philosophical Analysis*, 26–27, 35–40.

[21] Ibid., 39–40.

[22] Hick writes: "I hold that all conscious experience is interpretive in the sense that it has specific meaning for us in virtue of the concepts which function in the process by which it is brought to consciousness. I am thus in agreement at this point with Steven Katz in his influential paper 'Language, Epistemology, and Mysticism' [in *Mysticism and Philosophical Analysis*]" (*IR*, 169 n. 2).

[23] Katz, *Mysticism and Philosophical Analysis*, 4, 58.

[24] The diversity of contrary religious views does not of itself undermine the cognitivity of those views, even if all those views should prove false, since cognitivity has to do not with the *actual* truth or falsity a view but with whether it may validly be thought to be *possibly* true or false. One may be tempted to take up a skeptical view concerning *all* such views and deny that they are cognitive because of their wide diversity and inconsistency. It is an easy, though invalid step, from religious skepticism to the claim that religious language is noncognitive.

[25] Hick's writings on the theology of religions include: "Theology's Central Problem" (1967, in *GUF*); CC (1970); "The Reconstruction of Christian Belief" (1970, in *GUF*); "The Outcome: Dialogue into Truth" (1970), in *Truth and Dialogue in World Religions: Conflicting Truth-Claims*, ed. John Hick (Philadelphia: The Westminster Press, 1974); the Carrs Lane Church Centre Lectures of 1972: "The Essence of Christianity," "The Copernican Revolution in Theology," and "The New Map of the Universe of Faiths" (in *GUF*); "Whatever Path Men Choose is Mine" (1974, in *GHMNUK*) and, under the new title "By Whatever Path. . . " (in *GHMNUS*); *GUF* (1973); *DEL* (1976); "Christian Theology and Inter-Faith Dialogue" (1977, in *GHMNUK* and *GHMNUS*); "Christ in a Universe of Faiths" ([1977] (Leicester, UK: Quaker Universalist Group Pamphlet 3, 1983); "Present and Future Life" (1977, in *PRP*); "Eschatological Verification Reconsidered"

(1977, in *PRP*); "Jesus and the World Religions" (1977, in *MGI*); *GHMNUK* (1980); *GHMNUS* (1982); *PRP* (1985); "The Non-Absoluteness of Christianity" (1987, in *MCU*); "Trinity and Incarnation in the Light of Religious Pluralism," in *Three Faiths—One God: A Jewish, Christian, Muslim Encounter*, John Hick and Edmund S. Meltzer, eds. (Albany: State University of New York Press, 1989); *Disputed Questions in Theology and the Philosophy of Religions* (New Haven: Yale University Press, 1993); *The Metaphor of God Incarnate: Christology in a Pluralistic Age* (Louisville, KY: Westminster/John Knox Press, 1993).

[26] An example of this anachronistic understanding of Hick's position may be found in Gregory H. Carruthers, *The Uniqueness of Jesus in the Theocentric Model of the Christian Theology of Religions: An Elaboration and Evaluation of the Position of John Hick* (Lanham, MD: University Press of America, 1990). Although written too early to take into account *An Interpretation of Religion* (1989), there is no excuse for Carruthers not to be familiar with Hick's newer views, since they were first clearly articulated in a series of articles reprinted in *PRP* (1985), a volume which unaccountably is not included in Carruthers' bibliography. Carruthers either ignores Hick's later Real-centric philosophy of religions in favor of the earlier theocentric theology of religions or he is unaware of it. In either case, Carruthers' evaluation is a misrepresentation of Hick's position as Hick has articulated it since the early eighties. This is an especially serious fault in Carruthers' book, since he claims to be concerned with evaluating Hick's position, though his evaluation artificially emphasizes Hick's earlier theology of religions over Hick's later philosophy of religions. However, this violates the development one sees when viewing Hick's work as a whole, since Hick conceives his later Real-centered, post-Christian philosophy of religions as a corrective to the defects in his earlier theocentric Christian theology of religions. Carruthers is not alone in so failing to keep up with Hick's later thought on this topic, since Hick's name is still often associated with the theocentric Copernican revolution instead of with his recent work, which, as we will see later in this chapter, is inspired by a certain reading of the transcendental analytic of Kant's First Critique. Excepting Carruthers who has recently subjected Hick to criticism, this is an excusable fault, since not everyone can be expected to be familiar with Hick's latest work and because the Carrs Lane Lectures of 1972 (published as chapters 8–10 in *GUF*), in which Hick called for a Copernican revolution in religion, were so cogently argued and widely received that it will take some time for Hick's earlier position to recede in favor of his later position. Also, the widespread reception of the models of religious pluralism proposed by Paul Knitter in his widely read book *No Other Name: A Critical Survey of Christian Attitudes Toward the World Religions* (Maryknoll, NY: Orbis Books, 1985) reinforces this anachronistic view of Hick's position, since in Knitter's book Hick is cited as an exemplar of the theocentric model and as calling for a Copernican revolution in theology (146–152). Even in recent works on theology of religions this anachronistic reading of Hick persists,

which is due most likely to the influence of Knitter's book. See, for example, Clark H. Pinnock's, *A Wideness in God's Mercy: The Finality of Jesus Christ in a World of Religions* (Grand Rapids, MI: Zondervan Publishing House, 1992), 45–46 and John Sanders, *No Other Name: An Investigation into the Destiny of the Unevangelized* (Grand Rapids, MI: Eerdmans Publishing Company, 1992), 3. Although both of these writers, particularly Sanders, are aware of the later developments in Hick's thinking on religious pluralism (Pinnock, 46, 134–135; Sanders, 115–120), they give no evidence of knowing that Hick himself has abandoned theocentricity. Ronald H. Nash, an exclusivist theologian, in his popularizing account of current trends in theology of religions, *Is Jesus the Only Savior?* (Grand Rapids, MI: Zondervan Publishing House, 1994) draws attention, though inadequately and simplistically, to the change in Hick's views on religions. This lag in the interpretation of Hick by theologians and philosophers of religion ought in time to be remedied by Hick's *An Interpretation of Religion*, in which theocentrism and the Copernican revolution in theology are not so much as mentioned. However, Hick refers obliquely to the Copernican revolution in a recent article in which he returns to Christian theology of religions. The theology of religions of this article is theocentric, but is consistent with Hick's Real-centric philosophy of religions, since as Hick explains: "In this [article] I have been treating the question of the place of Christianity within the wider religious life of humanity as a topic *in Christian theology* [emphasis mine]. I have accordingly used our Christian term, God, to refer to the ultimate Reality to which, as I conceive, the great religious traditions constitute different human responses. But when one stands back from one's own tradition to attempt a philosophical interpretation of the fact of religious plurality one has to take full account of nonpersonal as well as of personal awarenesses of the Ultimate. I have tried to do this elsewhere, but it was not necessary to complicate this study, *as an intra-Christian discussion* [emphasis mine], in that way" ("The Non-Absoluteness of Christianity," *MCU*, 34).

[27] Hick's philosophy of religions was given its first detailed expression in "Toward a Philosophy of Religious Pluralism" (1980), in *GHMNUS*, although he first broached the distinction between a divine noumenon and divine phenomenon in "Mystical Experience as Cognition," in *Understanding Mysticism*, ed. Richard Woods (Garden City, NY: Doubleday, 1980), 429. In neither of these articles, however, had Hick yet hit upon the term *the Real*, still preferring *God* or *the Transcendent*, nor had he hit upon using the category-analogues, God and the Absolute. The notions of categories and schematism, however, are in place in the 1984 essay "A Philosophy of Religious Pluralism," reprinted in *PRP*. Hick's writings on the philosophy of religions also include: "Towards a Philosophy of Religious Pluralism" (1980, in *GHMNUS*); "Sketch for a Global Theory of Religious Knowledge" (1981, in *GHMNUS*); "On Grading Religions" (1982), "On Conflicting Religious Truth Claims" (1983), "In Defence of Religious Pluralism" (1983), "Seeing-as and Religious Experience" (1984), "A Philosophy of Religious Pluralism" (1984),

"Religious Pluralism and Absolute Claims" (1984), all reprinted in *PRP*; "Religious Diversity as Challenge and Promise," *The Experience of Religious Diversity*, ed. John Hick and Hasan Askari (Brookfield, VT: Gower Publishing, 1985); "Religious Pluralism," in *The Encyclopedia of Religion*, 331–333; *IR* (1989); "Straightening the Record: Some Response to Critics," *Modern Theology* 6 (January 1990); "A Response to Gerald Loughlin," *Modern Theology* 7 (1990): 57–66; *Disputed Questions in Theology and the Philosophy of Religions* (New Haven: Yale University Press, 1993); "Religious Pluralism and the Rationality of religious Belief," *Faith and Philosophy* 10 (1993): 242–49.

[28] Hick, *Truth and Dialogue in World Religions*, 151. Although published in 1974, *Truth and Dialogue in World Religions* is a collection of essays that were presented at the Conference on the Philosophy of Religion, which took place in April 1970 at the University of Birmingham.

[29] See *IR*, 236–238.

[30] A good explication of this is given by Hick in "Jesus and the World Religions" (*MGI*, 169).

[31] Hick, *IR*, 236–7. Hick first gives a list like this in *GUF*, 139–145. Variations of the list, with different orderings, omissions, or additions may be found in "Mystical Experience as Cognition," 428–9; *GHMNUS*, 91 ff.; *PRP*, 39–40; *IR*, 236–240. Gordon D. Kaufman introduces his distinction in *God the Problem* (Cambridge: Harvard University Press, 1972), 85–86, 95–100, 150, 169 n. 13.

[32] *Rg Veda*, 1.164.46. Hick explicitly quotes this passage to illustrate his view in *IR*, 252, 253, 275 n.1 and in *GUF*, 140.

[33] Heracleitus frag. 32 (trans. Freeman).

[34] Bernard J. Verkamp thinks that it "ironic for a pluralist like Hick to have so keen an appreciation for negative and positive interpretations of Ultimate Reality in Hindu and Buddhist theologies, and not be able to cultivate an appreciation for a similar polarity of thought within his own Christian tradition" ("Hick's Interpretation of Religious Pluralism," *International Journal for Philosophy of Religion* 30 [1991]: 112).

[35] However, the parallel between the two sets of conceptions is not complete, since the Hindu distinction refers to modes of ultimate reality (Brahman), while the Christian distinction refers to ways of using language about ultimate reality (God). The Hindu terms are ontologically oriented, while the Christian terms are epistemologically oriented. Despite this difference, the basic notion that reality is simultaneously effable and ineffable is supported by both sets of concepts.

[36] For Hick's position as expressed in this section, see *GUF*, chap. 9, "The Copernican Revolution in Theology."

[37] J. J. Lipner, "Does Copernicus Help? Reflections for a Christian Theology of

Religions," *Religious Studies* 13 (1977): 253. Keith Ward argues similarly, when he states that "I do not think one can hold a religious view [in Hick's sense of *religious* as opposed to *confessional*] without holding a confessional view of some sort, however attenuated and revised it may be. Any such view presupposes the truth of some basic religious beliefs—such as that there is a suprasensory realm, having a certain character, which actively discloses itself to humans" (*Religion and Revelation* [New York: Oxford University Press, 1994], 108).

[38] D'Costa, *John Hick's Theology of Religions,* 170, 184.

[39] Duncan B. Forrester, "Professor Hick and the Universe of Faiths," *Scottish Journal of Theology* 29 (1976): 69. Forrester's reference to "Vedantic Hindus" is vague, since there are both theistic and nontheistic interpretations of the *Vedānta-Sūtras,* which form part of the textual basis (*prasthānatraya*) of the various Vedāntic philosophies. It is clear that Forrester has in mind *advaitavāda,* or the nondual and nontheistic interpretation of Vedānta, as set forth by Śaṇkara. He seems to be unaware of those other major interpretations of Vedānta in which theism and modified forms of nondualism are prominent, as, most notably, in Rāmānuja's interpretation of Vedānta, which is known as *viśiṣṭādvaitavāda,* or the theory of qualified nondualism. This theory allows for a real, unsublatable, though not absolute difference to subsist between God and the individual soul.

[40] Lipner, "Does Copernicus Help?" 253; see also D'Costa, *John Hick's Theology of Religions,* where, following Lipner and Forrester, D'Costa argues that Hick's use of *God* is ambiguous, forcing Hick into an "either/or dilemma" between a theistic or a nontheistic interpretation of *God* (154). This same argument is made against this phase of Hick's thought by John Sanders in *No Other Name: An Investigation into the Destiny of the Unevangelized* (Grand Rapids, MI: William B. Eerdmans Publishing Company, 1992), 119–121.

[41] Forrester, "Professor Hick and the Universe of Faiths," 70.

[42] Originally published in 1980, it was reprinted as chapter 6 of *GHMNUS.* D'Costa confirms this dating of the shift in Hick's published views of other religions (*John Hick's Theology of Religions,* 153). Although off by a year ("Toward a Philosophy of Religious Pluralism" was published in 1980, as was the U.K. edition of *God has Many Names*), Hick also confirms that a basic change in his pluralistic hypothesis, such as replacing *God* with *the Real,* took place "in a number of articles and books published from 1981 onwards" ("Straightening the Record," 191).

[43] Hick has struggled to find a neutral term to refer to the "putative transcendent reality" (*IR,* 10). He finally opts for *the Real,* because, as he claims, "this term has the advantage that without being the exclusive property of any one tradition it is nevertheless familiar within all of them" (11). To back up this claim, he asserts that the term *the Real* is, *mutatis mutandis,* synonymous with the term *God,* (when

understood as neutral between personal and impersonal definitions), the Muslim term *al Ḥaqq,* the Sanskrit terms *sat* and *tattva,* the Chinese term *zhen.* (By taking these terms, although they arise in widely diverging cultural/linguistic contexts, as equivalent without any qualification, Hick writes as one though he were unaware of developments in the philosophy of language and philosophical hermeneutics since Heidegger and the later Wittgenstein. Hick also presses into service the Buddhist term *śūnyatā,* which, in his view, "is an anti–concept excluding all concepts [thus providing] a good symbol for the Real *an sich*" (246). Thus, in Hick's view, "'the Real' is . . . as good a generic name as we have for that which is affirmed in the varying forms of transcendent religious belief" (11).

[44] Lipner, "Does Copernicus Help?" 255.

[45] Hick explains why he turned to Kant: "It was above all Immanuel Kant, with his doctrine that we are necessarily aware of the world in terms of certain forms and categories inherent in the structure of unitary finite consciousness, who enabled the modern world to recognize the mind's own positive contribution to the meaningful character of its perceived environment" (*GHMNUS,* 103).

[46] Kant, *Critique of Pure Reason,* B306 (Kemp Smith, 267).

[47] Kant, *Critique of Pure Reason,* B307 (Kemp Smith, 268).

[48] This position is self-defeating, since it asserts something about that which it is asserted nothing can be asserted. That is, if the noumenal Real is unknowable, how can we even assert that it exists in the first place?

[49] Hick, *PRP,* 112; Hick and Michael Goulder, *Why Believe in God?* 33–34; *IR,* 246–7. Hick's noumenal Real is not an object or existent, but the environing whole—what in Sanskrit is called *sat,* "reality," "existence," or "being" (see 245, where Hick speaks of "the environing divine reality"). One has inescapably to do with the Real as a mechanic, a physicist, a biologist, and in whatever other roles human beings play. Each activity is grounded in a normative relation to distinct spheres or ranges of the Real. As Hick claims: "Our actions are appropriate or inappropriate not only in relation to our physical and social environments but also in relation to our ultimate environment, the Real" (351). In religion and philosophy, however, one may embrace the Real integrally, or holistically, by refusing to conceive the Real in terms of any element of finite experience. Despite this, the theologian and philosopher, in concession to the need of the human mind for clarifying analogies may conceive the Real in terms of some finite segment of the Real. The Real may thus be contracted by being conceived as nature, form, number, matter, a personal God, love, beauty, duty, service, sexuality, personhood, or as the whole of reality as far as it is known—all of which are *saguṇic* or cataphatic approaches (a brilliant analysis of this theme—the nullifying of metaphysics by identifying being with some selected portion of being rather than with the whole of being itself—is the subject of Étienne Gilson's *The Unity of Philosophical Expe-*

rience [New York: Charles Scribner's Sons, 1937]). Only by continually reminding oneself that the noumenal Real is forever beyond the whole as known—which is a *nirguṇic* or apophatic approach—can the mystery and utter transcendence of the noumenal Real be preserved as a limit concept for human thought and a goad for spiritual aspirations.

[50] Again, this position is self-defeating, for how can one assert about an unknowable *x* that it produces an "informational input"?

[51] Whether Hick avoids falling into what Kant called dialectical illusion by applying this reasoning to the noumenal Real rather than only to objects of the senses is a question one may ask Hick at this point. See Kant, *Critique of Pure Reason*, A63/B87–A64/B88, A296/B352–A298/B355, A580/B608–A583/B611.

[52] Hick also points out here that he is not ultimately concerned with questions of Kant interpretation, because that would distract attention from his purpose, which is to apply the distinction between noumena and phenomena to religion, a use that would have been rejected by Kant.

[53] Kant, *Critique of Pure Reason*, A249–250 and B306–307.

[54] Hick is exploiting a notorious ambiguity in Kant's exposition of the distinction between noumena and phenomena (*Critique of Pure Reason*, A236/B295–A260/B315). The difficulties associated with properly interpreting this section of the First Critique are immense and perhaps insoluble. For an excellent discussion of the merits of the various possible interpretations, see Henry E. Allison, *Kant's Transcendental Idealism: An Interpretation and Defense* (New Haven: Yale University Press, 1983), 237–254; see especially 247–254, where Allison discusses *"die heikle Frage der Affektion."* Hick must be placed within the camp of those realistic interpreters of Kant who oppose what Allison describes as "idealistic oriented followers and 'improvers' of Kant [who deny] that the *Critique* contains any doctrine of affection through things in themselves. This [idealistic] ploy, however, encounters two difficulties: (1) it is apparently contradicted by those passages in which it seems quite clear that Kant does recognize some sort of transcendental affection; and (2) it does not explain how empirical affection, that is, affection through empirical objects or appearances, can provide the necessary ground of our representations" (247). Michael Stoeber's critique of Hick's pluralistic hypothesis capitalizes on the inconsistency between Hick's "extreme constructivism," on the one hand, and his "position that the [noumenal] Real significantly impacts upon the mystic," on the other ("Constructivist Epistemologies of Mysticism" 111). Stoeber links this ticklish position of Hick to the equally ticklish position of Kant, who, according to Stoeber, thinks that "the noumenon has some effect upon the experiencing subject even though the categories are in constant play" (110).

[55] Hick attempts to avoid the dilemma of choosing between theistic and nontheistic interpretations of *God* by adopting the noumena/phenomena distinction and by

claiming that the personal and impersonal conceptions of deity are equally *phenomena:* "whilst there is a noumenal ground for the phenomenal divine attributes, this does not enable us to trace each attribute separately upwards into the Godhead or the Real. They represent the Real as both reflected and refracted within human thought and experience. But nevertheless the Real is the ultimate ground or source of those qualities which characterize each divine *persona* and *impersona* insofar as these are authentic phenomenal manifestations of the Real" (*IR* 247; see also 294–295). This move allows Hick to move beyond the familiar and vague proposal that the personal and nonpersonal conceptions are complementary in a full-bodied concept of the Real as well as the proposal that one or the other mode of conceiving the Real is more adequate than the other. Since both conceptions are equally phenomenal, neither can be chosen as true at the expense of the other. By calling both the personal and the impersonal conceptions of the Real phenomena, Hick leaves both in unsynthesized difference as mutually exclusive positions. (Hick does allow that *only on the level of phenomena* personal and impersonal conceptions of the Real are complementary (374). However, these notions, in Hick's view can have no "purchase" on the postulated noumenal Real (350).

[56] Hick, "Mystical Experience as Cognition," 429; see also 432–433; *IR*, 245, 246, 249.

[57] Kant does not dismiss the *possibility* that there may be some other mode of intuition than the sensible. It remains, in Kant's view, an open question whether a noumenon signifies a true object or is just the mere form of a concept. Only intellectual intuition, should there be such a faculty, could settle this question (*Critique of Pure Reason*, A252; see also A249, where Kant writes about things given *coram intuitu intellectuali*: "in the presence of intellectual intuition"). For analysis of this aspect of Kant's thought see Jonathan Bennett, *Kant's Analytic* (New York: Cambridge University Press, 1966), 55–60; see also *Kant's Transcendental Idealism*, 65, where Allison writes that "Kant claims that discursive knowledge is not the only conceivable kind of knowledge (although it is the only kind possible for man)." Kant expresses his ambivalence about intellectual intuition at A250–252 and B310. *In principle, if not in fact for human beings,* Kant tentatively holds open the *possibility* that there may be some direct awareness of noumena, an intuitive awareness "of a world which is thought as it were in the spirit" (A250). This ambiguity is reiterated by Kant in *The Critique of Judgement*, §77. This ambiguous position may be a holdover from Kant's precritical writings, as suggested by Keith Ward, "Truth and the Diversity of Religions," 11.

[58] Kant, *Critique of Pure Reason*, A250 (Kemp Smith, 267).

[59] Kant, *Critique of Pure Reason*, B307.

[60] This diagram revises D'Costa's diagram in *John Hick's Theology of Religions*, 160.

[61] *IR*, 202, 245, 246, 266, 350; on the ineffability of the noumenal Real, see 239; on the unity of the noumenal Real, see 248.

[62] Hick, "Mystical Experience as Cognition," 432; *IR*, 244–245. This notion is present in undeveloped form as early as Hick's first book, *Faith and Knowledge*, 1st ed. (Ithaca: Cornell University Press, 1957), where he writes that "in its most general form at least, we must accept the Kantian thesis that we can be aware only of that which enters into a certain framework of basic relations which is correlated with the structure of our own consciousness. These basic relations represent the minimal conditions of significance for the human mind" (112–113).

[63] Kant, *Critique of Pure Reason*, A96 (Kemp Smith, 130).

[64] Kant, *Critique of Pure Reason*, A66/B91 (Kemp Smith, 103).

[65] Kant, *Critique of Pure Reason*, A87/B119 (Kemp Smith, 121). Kant also wrote that "all intuitions, as sensible, rest on affections," and that "concepts are based on the spontaneity of thought, sensible intuitions on the receptivity of impressions" (*Critique of Pure Reason*, A68/B93 [Kemp Smith, 105]). These passages support a realistic reading of the First Critique. Nevertheless, this is a controversial reading of Kant, even if it seems to be supported by some passages in the First Critique. One may also read First Critique as intending, beyond all of Kant's vacillations (as evidenced in the chapter on phenomena and noumena [compare B309 with A260/B315]), a *holistic idealism* in which the ontological independence of noumena is reduced to zero (see Ward, "Truth and the Diversity of Religions," 11; J. N. Findlay, *Kant and the Transcendental Object: A Hermeneutic Study* [New York: Oxford University Press, 1981], 187).

[66] Findlay writes about "the problematically realistic character of Kantianism, and its remoteness from complete idealism" (*Kant and the Transcendental Object*, 15; see also 9–11). Kant writes "that we have *experience* and not merely imagination of outer things" (*Critique of Pure Reason*, B275 [Kemp Smith, 244]). Findlay's interpretation is at odds with holistic, a radical difference that indicates the difficulty of determining which of the two positions is ultimately justified as the *best* reading of the *Critique of Pure Reason*.

[67] The kind of intuition that Hick seems to be proposing is neither an unmediated intellectual intuition of noumena in themselves nor an intuition merely of objects of the external senses, but rather an intuition in which objects of the five senses and the "objects" of inner, religious experience are both constructed, since both kinds of objects are ultimately continuous with one another in the noumenal Real.

[68] *GHMNUS*, 105; *PRP*, 41; *IR*, 243, 245.

[69] These claims violate the supposed unknowability of the noumenal Real and also contradict Hick's earlier claim that the noumenal Real "impacts" human consciousness. Hick's thinking on this point is contradictory insofar as he holds that

the noumenal Real is both knowable and unknowable, both affective and neutral with respect to human consciousness.

[70] This trend in Hick's thought begins as early as his 1977 essay "Jesus and the World Religions" (in *MGI*) where Hick, perhaps as a consequence of the problems of conceiving the *verificandum,* suggests that a central Christian doctrine, the Incarnation, is a myth veiling a practical and not a literal truth. Hick writes, "that Jesus was God the Son incarnate is not literally true, since it has no literal meaning, but it is an application to Jesus of a mythical concept whose function is analogous to that of the notion of divine sonship ascribed in the ancient world to a king. In the case of Jesus it gives definitive expression to his efficacy as saviour from sin and ignorance and as giver of new life; it offers a way of expressing his significance to the world; and it expresses a disciple's commitment to Jesus as his personal Lord" (*MGI,* 178). As Hick progressed in his thinking, he came to the more radical conclusion that *all* religious doctrines and narratives are myths (*DEL* , 30; *IR,* 357).

[71] John Hick, "Religion as Fact-Asserting," in *A John Hick Reader,* ed. Paul Badham (Philadelphia: Trinity Press International, 1990), 15.

[72] Hick, "Theology's Central Problem," *GUF,* 2. Paradoxically, this view persists even in *An Interpretation of Religion* (in line with Hick's tendency to retain former positions alongside newer positions developed by him with which they conflict), where he claims that "in the case of Judeo-Christian-Islamic talk about God the realist [or cognitivist] assumption is that God exists as an unlimited personal being, so that in addition to all of the millions of embodied human consciousnesses there is at least one further consciousness which is not embodied and which is the divine consciousness" (*IR,* 173). Further evidence that Hick paradoxically retains this propositionalist/literalist view of the factuality of specific doctrines even as late as *An Interpretation of Religion* is seen in his attempt to base the factuality of Hinduism and Buddhism upon the possible eschatological verification of their specific eschatological doctrines (i.e., the universal realization of Brahman in the case of the Hindu school of Advaita Vedānta and entrance into *nirvāṇa* in the case of Buddhism (*IR,* 180–188). However, a problem develops if the eschatological doctrines of Buddhism, Hinduism, and Christianity and other religions are taken seriously as proposing possibly verifiable truth-claims, since these contrary doctrines cannot possibly all be true. As particular claims, the doctrines of *nirvāṇa* and Jesus' kingdom of God are inconsistent and only by a reductionistic syncretism of the kind practiced, for instance, by the perennialists, can they be equated.

[73] Hick restates this position in an 1987 lecture: "the different conceptions of the Real . . . are not literally true or false descriptions of the Real but are mythologically true insofar as they are soteriologically effective" (John Hick, "The Bud-

dha's Undetermined Questions and the Conflicting Truth Claims of Different Religions," in *Hermeneutics, Religious Pluralism, and Truth,* ed. Gregory D. Pritchard (Winston-Salem, NC: Wake Forest University, 1989), 16.

[74] Hick, *IR*, 355–6; see Plato, *Phaedo*, 114.

[75] *IR*, 343–59, 365–66; see also Hick, "The Buddha's Undetermined Questions and the Conflicting Truth Claims of Different Religions," 1–4.

[76] D'Costa discusses the relation in Hick's philosophy of religions between practical and theoretical defenses of religion, especially as regards the Buddhist view of this relation (*John Hick's Theology of Religions*, 178–180).

[77] However, there are a number of difficulties with this solution, which seem to rule out the possibility that Hick's pluralistic hypothesis is able to solve the difficulties for which it was conceived. It is circular to say that the mythic pictures of the noumenal Real are true insofar as they tend to elicit responses that are in soteriological alignment with the Real, since the only evidence offered by Hick for their truthfulness is the claim that they *are* in soteriological alignment with the noumenal Real. Also, with respect to the criterion of "practical truthfulness," which, in Hick's view consists in guiding us aright, one is compelled to ask what criterion is at work in the definition of *aright?*

4

A Critique of the Pluralistic Hypothesis

Objections to the Pluralistic Hypothesis

Reductionism and the Pluralistic Hypothesis

The pluralistic hypothesis is a reductionistic hypothesis insofar as it makes the truthfulness of religious doctrines and stories depend solely upon their power to orient human beings toward the unknowable and inexpressible noumenal Real. This hypothesis evacuates of content the doctrines and stories presented as true by the religious traditions by making their cognitivity depend solely upon their hypothetical power to orient human beings toward the merely formal and otiose concept of the noumenal Real. Thus, insofar as the systems of doctrines and cycles of stories that have gathered around, for instance, the names of Jesus, Buddha, or Kṛṣṇa orient one toward the noumenal Real they amount to the same thing: tokens for the noumenal Real, retaining no *relevant* differences and whose whole meaning is reduced to pragmatic efficiency in orienting their adherents to an unknowable, noumenal Real. This is an outcome that negates these diverse and specific doctrines and stories as cognitive *in their own right*. By reducing doctrines and stories to the status of ornamental metaphors for a more general soteriological process that is conceived as the transformation of the self's point of ultimate interest from self to the Real, the pluralistic hypothesis nullifies the significance of the doctrinal and narrative diversity of the religions.

Hick admits as much when, in his later writings, he claims that the doctrinal differences between religions are not "soteriologically vital" (*IR*, 367).[1] Unlike the younger Hick,[2] the older Hick now views doctrines as a kind of "secondary" packaging and labeling.[3] Clearly, Hick is here subordinating what is different between the religions to what he thinks is common to them.[4] As a particularist theologian notes by way of protest: "in his latest works, Hick reinterprets all religions . . . in an effort to place them all within the same framework as mythological responses to 'the Real.'"[5]

This reinterpretation of religious doctrines and stories as merely the culturally variable packaging, or tokens of different shapes and colors, of the one noumenal reality, secures a formal and vacuous assurance of the cognitivity of the doctrines and stories of religious traditions at the expense of their concrete, substantive particularity. It does this by its insistence that the noumenal Real is the true goal or intention of the stories and doctrines of the various traditions. However, such a thin concept as the noumenal Real can muster little devotion or warrant little credence from those whose religious lives are lived within one of the rich webs of practice, belief, and tradition that constitute the religious traditions.

This is a serious fault of the pluralistic hypothesis since not many adherents of specific religions would likely, upon reflection, agreeably allow their beliefs, or interpretation of the mystery of existence, to be subjected to the reductionism inherent in Hick's pluralistic hypothesis.[6] Nor would they likely agree that the noumenal Real is the *true* intention of the various vocabularies that they employ in their dealings with the mystery of existence.

Supporting this view is Kenneth Surin, who contends that Hick's pluralistic hypothesis is a Procrustean bed that "regiments or 'irons out' the somewhat messy, idiosyncratic, and recalcitrant historico-cultural features of the particular religions."[7] By abandoning the "unique material content of each religion"[8] (i.e., their interpretations of existence), the pluralistic hypothesis traduces "the 'otherness' of the Other" and extinguishes "the real possibility of any kind of dialectical confrontation between the different religious traditions."[9] This approach, according to Surin, undermines the possibility of getting better interpretations that are regulated by the ethical principle of mutuality, or openness to the many sorts of others that inhabit the planet. Surin thinks that Hick, despite his stated constructivist concerns with preserving the irreducible uniqueness of the religions, lacks insight

> into the central problematic which confronts anyone who is concerned about the relation between religion and truth: namely, how can something enduring and ineffable (which is what truth itself is), emerge from something sensuous and time-bound (which is what religion is)?[10]

That is, Hick ignores the particularity and historicity of the individual traditions. Despite constructivist appearances, Hick thus turns out to a crypto-perennialist.

Just before his death in 1923, Ernst Troeltsch wrote presciently of the situation in which philosophy of religions now inescapably finds itself. Troeltsch opposed attempts to homogenize or to subordinate any of the historically diverse religions to another religion (such as Christianity) when he claimed that the element of truth in every religion "can only be disentangled through strife and disruption."[11] This strife is inherent in the dialogue of competing interpretations of religious life offered by the many religions and their variants. Troeltsch, like Surin, but unlike Hick, was not willing to see the study of religion turn away from this rivalry of conflicting, materially conditioned embodiments of truth, or interpretations, since Troeltsch believed that only this rivalry could lead to "the attainment of interior purity and clearness of vision" in each of the religions that would lead to the richest expression of the "Divine life" within the unpredictable and uncontainable flux of history.[12]

Hick offers his pluralistic hypothesis partly in order to avoid the strife and controversy instigated by competing religious interpretations,[13] which he thinks, are not conducive to harmony and peace in a world rapidly becoming one, and partly out of a desire to redeem the West, and Christianity in particular, from the imperialist assumption that it has the final interpretation—the final truth—to offer other cultures and religions (*MCU*, 17–20). These are noble motivations and much to be applauded. Nevertheless, most adherents of most religions will see the pluralistic hypothesis not only as reductionistic and thus derogatory to the visions of religious truth to which they adhere, but also as another form of Western or Christian religious reinterpretation and reduction to foreign assumptions of what they hold as the deepest truths of life.[14]

Furthermore, the attempt to rule out differences between and controversy among the religions by means of the device of the pluralistic hypothesis is intellectually immodest, for it evinces—certainly unintentionally on Hick's part—an omniscience that can all too easily degenerate into a totalizing quasi perennialism. To escape the consequences of such an interpretation of religions, adherents of religious traditions will likely continue to believe that the cognitive content of their religious traditions is to be found in their traditional interpretations of the mystery of life and not in a nebulous reference to a postulated Real that is beyond all knowledge and experience.[15]

Theological Arrogance and the Pluralistic Hypothesis

In response to Hick's recent writings on the pluralistic hypothesis, a number of particularist Christian theologians of religions have argued that dissent from Hick's position is not only philosophically reasonable but also theologically necessary if Christian faith is to retain its own integrity. A glance at the views put forward in books by two Christian particularists, the inclusivist Lesslie Newbigin and the exclusivist Harold A. Netland, will illustrate this vigorous resistance to Hick's post-Copernican religious pluralism.

Newbigin spent over forty years as a Christian missionary in India, is fluent in Tamil, and is deeply knowledgeable of Hinduism. In his book *The Gospel in a Pluralist Society*, he rejects religious pluralism as advocated by such writers as Gordon D. Kaufman, Wilfred Cantwell Smith, Paul Knitter, Diana Eck, and John Hick.[16] Newbigin proposes a position that, in contrast to the views of these writers, is "pluralist in the sense of acknowledging the gracious work of God in the lives of all human beings, but it rejects a pluralism which denies the uniqueness and decisiveness of what God has done in Jesus Christ" (182–83).

With Hick particularly in mind, Newbigin turns to a criticism of the kind of pluralism that he rejects, a pluralism that turns "the true statement that none of us can grasp the whole truth" into "an excuse for disqualifying any claim to have a valid clue for at least the beginnings of understanding [what Hick calls the Real *an sich*]" (169–70). Newbigin sees this position as an "appearance of humility" that actually veils "an arrogant claim to a kind of knowledge which is superior to the knowledge which is available to fallible human beings" (170). He then tries to cut to the root of this covertly immodest, infallibilist pluralism by turning the pluralists' denial of an infallible knowledge grounded upon a superior vantage point of insight upon its head. He asks the pluralist how he or she *knows* that the truth about God is greater than what is revealed to human beings in Jesus? What is the *higher* truth, the *vantage ground*, that allows the pluralist to relativize the claims made by Christian and other scriptures in light of an unknowable "Reality" that cannot be identified with any specific religious name, form, image or, story (170)? Newbigin is unwilling to take this nebulous "Reality" in place of the specific traditional Christian affirmation that salvation is possible because God has acted in the "historical person of the man Jesus" to take from human beings the burden of sin and to invite them to trust in him so that their lives will center not in the self but in God (169).

Hick's pluralistic hypothesis cannot make room for Newbigin's faith *as it stands* and that of classical Christians who believe as Newbigin does. By forcing a choice between clear, traditional teaching and an innovation that evacuates the traditional teaching of specific content and offers a meager return for such a great sacrifice, the pluralistic hypothesis, in Newbigin's view, is an arrogant and arbitrary assault upon classical Christian doctrine.

Another recent defender of Christian particularism is Harold A. Netland, who was a student of John Hick's at Claremont and went on to become an Evangelical Free Church missionary in Japan and an assistant professor at Tokyo Christian University. Against the pluralism advocated by Hick and others, he candidly argues for Christian *exclusivism*, as formulated in the first Lausanne Covenant of 1974:

> We . . . regard as derogatory to Christ and the gospel every kind of syncretism and dialogue which implies that Christ speaks equally through all religions and ideologies. Jesus Christ, being the only God-man, who gave himself as the only ransom for sinners, is the only mediator between God and man. There is no other name by which we must be saved.[17]

Writing from the standpoint of this covenant, Netland summarizes Christian exclusivism as involving the four following claims:

> (a) Jesus Christ is the unique Incarnation of God, fully God and fully man; (b) only through the person and work of Jesus Christ is there any possibility of salvation; (c) the Bible is God's unique revelation written, and thus is true and authoritative; and (d) where the claims of Scripture are incompatible with those of other faiths, the latter are to be rejected as false.[18]

Netland is what I would call a *weak exclusivist*,[19] since he *does not* reject as false those doctrines of other religions that are *consis-*

tent with Christian doctrine, such as, for instance, the agreement between classical Christianity and theistic forms of Hinduism that God is both personal and gracious. He also points out that exclusivism is not exclusively Christian, but that Christian exclusivism is only one example of religious exclusivism. Every religious tradition is exclusivist insofar as one of its central beliefs is that the central affirmations of its own faith are true and that claims of other religions that are incompatible with its own claims are false.[20] Examples of exclusivism outside of Christianity are the Theravāda Buddhist rejection of the Christian doctrine of an absolute, supreme, creator God, the Islāmic rejection of the Christian doctrine that Jesus Christ was God incarnate, and the Advaita Vedāntic rejection of any ultimate difference between Brahman and individual souls, or *jīvas*. This impels Netland to reject Hick's reductionistic evacuation of the *content* of the doctrines and stories of these diverse religious communities, which results from seeing them as mythical tokens of the noumenal Real whose truth is determined pragmatically and soteriologically. Netland writes:

> Hick's treatment of various beliefs is frequently reductionistic and he freely interprets troublesome doctrines so as to accommodate them within his theory. But to the extent that major religious traditions do not find their beliefs—as they are understood within the respective traditions— adequately accounted for on Hick's analysis, his theory is called into question.[21]

Netland points out that the pluralistic hypothesis fails seriously to take into account that each of the major traditions "ascribes ultimacy to its own particular conception of the religious ultimate."[22] Consequently, the pluralistic hypothesis discounts the central doctrines of religious communities, a failing that "counts against his theory."[23] The claim that Yahweh, Dharmakāya, the Tao, Jesus Christ, Amida Buddha, and Brahman are penultimate manifestations of the ultimate unknowable noumenal Real and not the very content of ultimate reality itself would be vigorously resisted by the adherents of each these various conceptions of the divine.[24] Thus, from the standpoint of the religious traditions themselves the strife of doctrines is unavoidable.[25]

The Real *an sich:* Transcendental or Causal?

At times Hick characterizes the Real *an sich* in transcendental terms, calling it, for instance, a "necessary postulate":

> If the Real in itself is not and cannot be humanly experienced, why postulate such an unknown and unknowable *Ding an sich?* The answer is that the divine noumenon is a necessary postulate of the pluralistic life of humanity.... we are led to postulate the Real *an sich* as the presupposition of the veridical character of this range of forms of religious experience (*IR*, 249).

In Hick's view the appending of this postulate to otherwise neutral or nonreligious phenomenological accounts of the life of religious communities transforms these accounts into *religious* interpretations, thus distinguishing them from nonreligious, noncognitive, and functional interpretations of religion. This postulate thus offers an alternative, on behalf of the religions themselves, to the totalizing aspirations of nonreligious, noncognitive, and nonfunctional interpretations of religion.[26] The point of Hick's transcendental appeal to the cognitively empty postulate of the noumenal Real is to prevent noncognitive or functionalist explanatory or interpretive strategies—whether they emerge from within religious studies or from external disciplines—from negating or ignoring the essential reliance of lived religion and religious interpretations of religion upon a transcendent divine reality. Thus, Hick writes:

> We have postulated the Real as the ground of this varied realm of religious phenomena. Indeed we have already committed ourselves to such a

postulate in rejecting the view of religious experience as simply human projection (*IR*, 350).[27]

Hick is not consistent in holding to this *transcendental* conception of the noumenal Real, since he also conceives the noumenal real as an element in the *causal* complex that generates religious experience. Thus, he writes: "all that we are entitled to say about the noumenal [Real] . . . is that it is the reality whose influence produces, in collaboration with the human mind, the phenomenal world of our experience" (*IR*, 243).

However, causality cannot be predicated of a transcendental postulate, which is a merely notional entity. That is, if the noumenal Real is a causal agent, it cannot at the same time be a transcendental postulate. The difference between these two positions is striking and, it would seem, unbridgeable.

Yet Hick not only slides back and forth between these contrary ways of conceiving the noumenal Real, he often conflates them in the same sentence or paragraph, thereby creating an unanalyzed confusion of transcendental and causal conceptions of the noumenal Real. Hick claims, quite paradoxically, that

> the Real *an sich* is *postulated* by us as a pre-supposition . . . of religious experience and [of] the religious life, whilst the gods, as also the mystically known Brahman, Sunyata, and so on, are phenomenal *manifestations* of the Real occurring within the realm of religious experience (*IR*, 243, emphases mine).[28]

It is not consistent to claim with respect to a supposedly *transcendental* entity such as the Real *an sich* that it has *manifestations*, that it *effects* schematizations *of itself*, in concert with human cognitive processes and culture, within the realm of religious experience. Nor does it make sense to claim that an unexperienced *transcendental* postulate "*impacts*" human consciousness, as Hick does:

> Since we can never experience the unexperienced [the noumenal Real] we can never compare the world as it appears in consciousness with the *pos-*

tulated world as it exists independently of its *impacts* upon our human sensory and nervous systems (*IR*, 134–35, emphases mine).

Although conceptual precision requires carefully distinguishing between these two conceptions, Hick haphazardly throws them together, as when he writes about "the *postulated presence* of the Real to human life of which it is the *ground*" (*IR*, 244, emphasis mine).[29] This same conceptual imprecision is seen in a passage from an older writing of Hick's on this topic, in which he addresses the skeptical question that arises about a postulated unknowable *x*:

> If the ultimate divine Reality can be humanly known only in various imperfect and culturally conditioned ways, on what grounds can we claim that behind these varied religious phenomena lies an unexperienceable divine noumenon? The basic answer is that we *postulate* that noumenon in affirming the basic conviction that religious experience is not, as such, an illusory projection of our imaginations. The conviction that religious experience is not *caused* solely by human factors, but also by the *impact* upon us of a transcendent Reality, leads to the theory of an ultimate divine noumenon which is humanly known as a range of divine phenomena (*PRP*, 106, emphases mine).

The first two sentences of this quote are consistent with Hick's transcendental use of the concept of the noumenal Real, though if we were to replace the word *conviction* with *faith* we would see that the postulate functions less as a piece of a transcendental deduction of the cognitivity of religions and more as a confession of faith in the face of nonbelievers of the validity of what one believes, though there is no commonly accepted procedure of demonstrating its veridicality. However, in the last sentence Hick introduces a perplexing twist into his argument by claiming a *causal* role (i.e., "impact") for the divine noumenon in the production of religious experience. How something to which the notion of cause does not apply can have an impact is not at all clear to me. Furthermore, the conception of the noumenal Real as a postulate collapses completely in this last sentence when Hick implies that the postulate of the divine noumenon is *empirically induced* from the various impacts producing the range of phenomenal expressions of the Real *an sich*.[30] To claim that a transcendental postulate is a product of an empirical doctrine is to verge on incoherence. As a nonempirical concept whose function is to distinguish between otherwise identical religious and nonreligious interpretations of religion, the noumenal Real can be neither the veiled object nor the partial cause of religious experience. It cannot affect, like a wall or a drug, the human sensory and nervous system. All that it can do is to give a spurious speculative, theoretical assurance to the one who has religious experience that such experience is not an illusion.

The most fundamental question to address to Hick at this point is: Does he intend that the noumenal Real should be understood as simply an entity necessitated by the transcendental logic of his quasi-Kantian reliance upon the noumenon/phenomenon distinction, which then serves as the sole guarantor of the cognitivity of religions? Or does he intend that the noumenal Real be understood as a partial cause, along with the biological processes of cognition and also of culture, of religious experience?[31]

If Hick holds that the noumenal Real is only an element in a transcendental logic justifying *a priori* a religious over against a nonreligious interpretation of religions, then it is subject to all of the problems noted here and elsewhere in this chapter. If, on the other hand, Hick sees the noumenal Real as a *causal* factor in the generation of religious experience, then his position, as I will argue in the next chapter, would be a defensible one (though he would have to drop the quasi-Kantian term *noumenal*, with its residual implication of the untenable noumenon/phenomenon distinction), one that can find support in traditional mystical interpretations of the diversity of religious experience. This postulate would involve a return to the standard mystical distinction that Hick held to before Kantianizing it.[32]

The Ineffability of the Noumenal Real

Another difficulty with the pluralistic hypothesis arises from Hick's understanding of ineffability. When he writes that "our language can have no purchase on a postulated noumenal reality which is not even partly formed by human concepts" (*IR*, 350), he is proposing a version of "strong ineffability,"[33] or the idea that no concepts apply to the noumenal Real. As Keith Ward cogently argues, this position is far more radical than the traditional doctrine of ineffability, as elaborated, for instance, by Thomas Aquinas.[34] As even Hick recognizes, strong ineffability has been criticized as incoherent because it involves the impossible attempt to refer to something that supposedly does not even have the property of "being able to be referred to." However, Hick dismisses this criticism of strong ineffability as a logical pedantry (*IR*, 239).

Rather than retreat to a more modest doctrine of ineffability, Hick tries to neutralize this logical pedantry by drawing a distinction between logical and substantial properties. He then claims that such substantial properties as "being good," "being powerful," and "having knowledge" do not apply to the noumenal Real (*IR*, 239), while such "purely and logically generated properties" as "being a referent of a term" and "being that to which our substantial concepts do not apply" do apply to the noumenal reality (*IR*, 239, 246, 352).

However, this appears to be an unworkable view, since we don't seem to be able to say anything at all about that to which *no* substantial properties apply. Without the help of substantial properties, there is no way we can identify that to which the logical properties supposedly apply. Indeed, even the so-called logical properties that Hick proposes, such as "being a referent of a term," turn out to be substantial properties in disguise. As Keith Ward points out in cogently arguing this point: to say that "X is to be used as a noun" is to say what sort of term X is without saying what real thing X might refer to. But to say that "X is the referent of some noun" is to make a synthetic proposition about some identifiable object, rather than just to give a formal property of a term. X has at least one property, when it is the referent of some noun: it is identifiable. Thus, the distinction between logical and substantial predicates cannot be used to support the view that the noumenal Real can be spoken of only in terms of formal properties to the exclusion of all substantial properties. Ward illumines this futile situation with the analogy of doing logic with nothing but p's and q's: one can go on for days setting out argument-forms without ever uttering an argument.[35] Yet this empty activity illustrates what Hick's doctrine of the noumenal Real amounts to: it is a formal placeholder, empty of all content, incongruously taken as the superexcellent ground and referent of all the substantial properties that the religions ascribe to their divine realities.

A striking example of this is Hick's claim that such attributes as love, justice, bliss, consciousness, and so forth do not apply to the noumenal Real, even though it is the infinitely rich ground of all these properties (*IR*, 247). This is a far more radical doctrine of ineffability than that proposed even by such a radical ineffabilist as Dionysius the Areopagite (*c.* 500). In the very last phrase of the *Mystical Theology*, after piling up negation upon negation, Pseudo-Dionysius, finally negates negation itself, when he ecstatically exclaims that the cause of all things is "free from every limitation and beyond them all."[36] The terminus of the *via negativa*, Pseudo-Dionysius abruptly but with absolute propriety points out, is also the terminus of the *via affirmativa*. In contrast, Hick's radical, unbalanced apophaticism fails to acknowledge the unity of the two ways in their ultimate terminus (*IR*, 247). Keith Ward also renders the same judgment; he asserts that Hick "has taken the doctrine of the *via negativa* out of relation to its complementary doctrine of *via eminentia* to produce the new doctrine that the Real *an sich* is wholly unknowable."[37] Hick's failure to recognize the essential complementarity of these two ways of using theological language leads to the incoherence of the pluralistic hypothesis.[38]

Thus Hick, seeking by the use of a merely formal device to secure the cognitivity of religion, actually makes religious cognitivity hang upon one slender thread: reference to the noumenal Real. However, when the incoherence of the notion of the noumenal Real is seen, this slender thread is cut, and the religions fall unwillingly to the ground, where they are prey to roving bands of noncognitivist theologians and interpreters of religions. The pluralistic hypothesis, then, comes to a dead-end as a defense of religious cognitivity. Indeed, it terminates—contrary to Hick's intentions in developing the pluralistic hypothesis—in another version of religious noncognitivism, for apart from the unsubstantiatable claim that the noumenal Real exists, Hick's view of religion immediately collapses into the noncognitivist, nonreligious, and functionalist interpretations of religion that the pluralistic hypothesis is designed to counteract.[39] No way remains for Hick on his own terms to distinguish between noncognitive, though ethically sensitive, nonreligious interpretations and cognitive religious interpretations of religion, which is one of Hick's main intentions in writing *An Interpretation of Religion.*[40]

The Otioseness of the Noumenal Real

Critics of Hick's pluralistic hypothesis have been quick to point out that the noumenal Real is otiose—it does no real work in Hick's hypothesis—and is thus an excisable appendage. Stephen Grover in one of the first reviews of *An Interpretation of Religion* writes that "if it is by their ethical and spiritual fruits *alone* that the various religions are to be evaluated" (that is, by the soteriological criterion), then the metaphysical underpinning provided for the pluralistic hypothesis "by the nebulous notion of the Real seems to be doing no work."[41] From this observation, it follows that the noumenal Real is "ontologically unnecessary,"[42] as Gerald Loughlin claims.

If the noumenal Real is otiose, then one is left with no compelling reason why one should accept its existence. Like Locke's matter and Kant's noumena, Hick's divine noumenon may simply be dispensed with by anyone who thinks that it is an arbitrary construction. If one takes this stance towards the noumenal Real, then it becomes apparent that this notion is useless, despite Hick's intentions, as a protection of religious interpretations of religions against reduction to nonreligious interpretations.

The Relativity of Hick's Categories

A further difficulty with the pluralistic hypothesis is that while Kant's categories are universal and necessary, Hick's are culture-relative, as he himself admits. Furthermore, Hick thinks that people can choose which category, God or Absolute, that they want to use to relate themselves to the noumenal Real. This belief goes completely against the understanding of a Kantian category, which is universal and necessary and allows no scope for human volition as to its place in the construction of knowledge (*IR*, 244).[43]

The Redundancy of Schematization

Related to this quite un-Kantian understanding of a category is Hick's claim that his two basic religious categories, God and the Absolute, are schematized, or concretized, within actual religious experience as the variety of gods and absolutes worshipped in the religious traditions. Schematization for Kant serves to temporalize

what are thought by him to be universal and necessary dispositions of the understanding, while for Hick, the concepts of God
and Absolute are *already* temporalized, that is, they are "culture
relative" (*IR*, 9) Schematization is, thus, redundant in Hick's hypothesis, since the concepts God and Absolute are already temporalized. That is, they are not universal and necessary concepts,
inherent in all human understanding, but are products of various
cultures, just as their supposed concretizations as Allāh, Kṛṣṇa,
Brahman, and so forth are products of various cultures.

The Turn to a Pragmatic Criterion

Given these theoretical difficulties, it is not surprising that
Hick tries to push the pluralistic hypothesis in two contrary direc-
tions at the same time. On the one hand, Hick wants to ground the
cognitivity of religions by developing new categories of theoretical
reason, while, on the other hand, he wants to justify the cognitivity of religions by turning to practical reason, in the form of the
soteriological criterion.[44] This latter, practical, tendency is at odds
with the former, theoretical tendency, which inspired Hick's elaborate attempt in *An Interpretation of Religion* to construct an epistemology of religion based on a radical modification of Kant's transcendental analytic that would make it able to account for the
construction not only of physical but of hyperphysical realities.
Thus, despite Hick's high metaphysical ambition of guaranteeing
the cognitivity of the religions by postulating the noumenal Real,
he is forced by the various theoretical difficulties mentioned above
to give supremacy to practical reason. In so doing, Hick consciously takes a page from Buddhist dialectics (*IR*, 343–47).

Early Buddhist philosophy marked out four areas in which
unanswerable metaphysical disputes arose: whether the world is
or is not eternal; whether the world is or is not spatially infinite;
whether the soul (*jīva*) is or is not identical with the body, and

whether perfectly enlightened beings exist, do not exist, both exist and do not exist, or neither exist nor do not exist after death? These speculative metaphysical issues (*ditthi*) were said by the Buddha to be irresolvable and inexpressible (*avyakāta*) (*IR*, 343–47). Consequently, for Hick, following the example of the Buddha, the resolution of such issues is irrelevant to the practical issue of living right with respect to the Real and to other human beings. As Hick writes:

> I have argued that each of the great traditions constitutes a context and, so far as human judgment can at present discern, a more or less equally effective context, for the transformation of human existence from self-centredness to Reality-centredness. Accordingly, *it does not seem to make any soteriological difference* whether one believes that the world is or is not eternal and its history cyclical or linear, that we do or do not reincarnate, that there are or are not angels and devils and a hierarchy of heavens and hells (*IR*, 369, emphasis mine).[45]

As useful as this conclusion may be on the practical level, a ticklish theoretical issue remains. By reducing religious cognitivity to a generalization about the more or less equal pragmatic and soteriological effects of contrary doctrines, Hick's approach neatly sidesteps the whole issue of whether the various stories and claims about Buddha, Jesus or Kṛṣṇa are meaningful *as they stand*, providing essential soteriological knowledge available nowhere else. What we get instead is the *theoretically unhelpful* suggestion that each of these stories and claims is true or false insofar as it turns one from self toward reality. Thus, in the pluralistic hypothesis, the meaningful (or cognitive) element of the many religions, despite their doctrinal and narrative diversity, can be reduced to one sentence: does this story or doctrine conduce to the overcoming of egoism and the turn toward the Real?

Viewed in this perspective, Hick seems to be developing a new form of perennialism, despite his stated allegiance to constructivism. All of the possibilities of divine self-expression latent within the flux of history become irrelevant for the pluralistic hypothesis, which despite Hick's pledge of fealty to constructivism, becomes as vacuous and ahistorical a reductionism as perennialism through its reduction of religious cognitivity to soteriological efficacy. Although avoiding the perennialists' phenomenological reduction of religion to a common experience, the pluralistic hypothesis involves a pragmatic reduction of the concrete content of religions, since what counts as the criterion of the truth of particular religious stories and doctrines is not their specific and conflicting contents but rather their efficiency at orienting the worshipper toward the noumenal Real. Thus, Hick repeats the error of the perennialists by slighting the concrete differences of the religions in favor of a criterion thought generally applicable to all *true* religions. That a tendency toward perennialism is implicit in the pluralistic hypothesis has also been noted by Bernard Verkamp. In noting this tendency, Verkamp points out that theologians Raimundo Pannikar and John Cobb "suspect that [Hick] is still searching for some 'universal theory' or 'common source' of religion."[46]

Given this outcome, one can only conclude that in order to avoid the narrowness of religious particularism Hick has paid too high a price: the sacrifice of the messy, living tissue of actual, ongoing religious traditions. With respect to religious noncognitivism, this approach also comes up short, for it places all of its bets on religious truth upon the slender threads of the transcendental postulate of the noumenal Real and the soteriological criterion. The first thread is broken when one recognizes the otioseness and dispensability of the noumenal Real. For then no intelligible difference remains between merely phenomenological or functional descriptions of religion and descriptions that depend upon the addition of the postulate of the noumenal Real to make them refer to a reality external to the language game and lifeworld of the religious tradition under study. The second thread of religious cognitivity is frayed nearly to the breaking point when the soteriological criterion is seen as reducing the truth about the rich diversity of religious doctrines and stories to a thin assertion about the ethical direction of a religion as a whole. The thread breaks when one realizes that this thin ethical assertion can be interpreted in nonreligious terms as the guiding principle of a nonreligious system of ethics. In these ways, then, the pluralistic hypothesis, which was designed as a defense against religious noncognitivism, plays into the very error it was designed to defeat.

The hard, stubbornly held, concrete beliefs of the religious traditions offer a much more defensible face to noncognitivism than the reductionistic pluralistic hypothesis, since they exist within the plausibility structures of living religions, and have been adhered to for millennia by untold numbers of people.[47] Against such tenacious beliefs, the claim of religious noncognitivists that religious doctrines and stories are *merely* functional, or symbolic of other human processes, whether social or psychological, is but one more belief or story that can only enter as one finite viewpoint in the universal conversation from which truth tentatively and sporadically emerges.

Conclusion

My rejection of Hick's quasi-Kantian pluralistic hypothesis is based on the reductionism and tendency toward a crypto-perennialism fostered by the hypothesis. Difficulties in making sense of the basic concepts of the hypothesis also play a role in my rejection of this approach to religious pluralism. Finally, the elevation of practical criteria over the theoretical defense of religious cognitivity is unsatisfactory. Although the determination of the *consequences* of doctrines and stories is indispensable to their evaluation, this sort of evaluation does not itself provide insight into the *meaning* of doctrines and stories, since the latter have meanings that are independent of their consequences. For example, one may believe in the benevolence of a supreme deity, even though one has lived a life wracked with suffering, want, and loss. To identify meaning with consequences is to fall into the error of cognitive equivalence (see appendix).

Since Hick's intention of preserving the belief in the cognitivity of religions, despite the welter of unassimilable beliefs, stories, and practices that each tradition venerates is, I believe, unimpeachable, it would be a merely negative and destructive undertaking to end my study of Hick at this point. When Hick crossed the theological Rubicon by making God and later the Real the object of religion rather than Jesus, he compelled Christian theology, both revisionist and evangelical, to come to terms with its inherent bias toward the ultimacy of Christianity and revelation in Christ. Revisionist theologians, whether they agreed with Hick or not, were quick to respond to his theological Copernicanism. Throwing off the baleful influence of Barth and Hendrik Kraemer, they reevaluated Christian teaching in this area, with the result that now it is becoming rarer for revisionist theologians to make any sweeping, universal claims for Christianity or revelation in Christ. In response to Hick, some evangelical theologians, though refusing to cross the Rubicon of decentering Jesus, have moved away from harsh exclusivism and denigration of other religions to a wider vision of Christian inclusivism and humility in the face of the mystery of human religiosity and piety in its myriad expressions.

Although one may disagree with much of what Hick has written, one cannot deny that he has been a powerful force behind the recent rethinking of the place of Christianity in the universe of faiths. Long after his writings on verificationism are forgotten, it is likely that he will still be remembered as one of the first Christian theologians who boldly led a revolution that promises the advent of a future version of Christianity that knows how to be faithful to the truth that it discovers in Jesus while remaining at ease with the recognition that Jesus is an important but not the only or final word about the mysteries of life, death, and what falls in between. In *The Metaphor of God Incarnate: Christology in a Pluralistic Age*, Hick suggests an outlook that could animate a cosmically decentered, yet still vital Christianity. Speaking as a Christian to Christians, he writes:

> The alternative [to Christian particularism] is a Christian faith which takes Jesus as our supreme (but not necessarily only) spiritual guide; as our personal and communal lord, leader, guru, exemplar, and teacher, but not as literally himself God; and which sees Christianity as one authentic context of salvation/liberation amongst others, not opposing but interacting in mutually creative ways with the other great paths. . . . a non-traditional Christian faith can be genuinely simple and yet profound. Consider the belief that there is an ultimate transcendent Reality which is the source and ground of everything; that this reality is benign in relation to human life; that the universal presence of this Reality is reflected ("incarnated") in human terms in the lives of the world's great spiritual leaders; and that amongst these we [Christians] have found Jesus to be our principal revelation of the Real and our principal guide for living. This is basic religious faith in Christian form. It is our human response to the mystery of the universe, powered by religious experience and guided by rational thought.[48]

Out of respect, then, for the work that Hick has done on the issue of religious pluralism, I will now propose an alternative to the pluralistic hypothesis, one which might have come from Hick's own pen had Hick not inexplicably taken a turn toward Kant's First Critique, but, rather, had chosen to develop his pluralistic hypothesis in terms of ideas that have, unlike his quasi-Kantian notions, always been at the center of his thought: the cognitive ambiguity of the universe, human cognitive freedom, faith as interpretation, and the rationality of trusting one's own experience.

Notes

[1] On this point, Hick writes: "It can hardly be necessary for salvation/liberation, even from a theistic point of view, to know whether the universe is eternal. . . . To believe that the universe is or is not eternal cannot significantly help or hinder the transformation of human existence from self-centredness to Reality-centredness" (*IR*, 367).

[2] Hick maintained the fact-asserting character of specific theological doctrines prior to the development of the pluralistic hypothesis. As Julius Lipner, writing about the younger Hick, states: "Hick holds that religious truth-claims are indeed fact asserting and therefore that they ought to be verifiable in some way or other" ("Truth-Claims and Inter-Religious Dialogue," *Religious Studies* 12 [1976]: 220). Lipner bases this claim on a reading of Hick's 1960 article "Theology and Verification" (*EG*, 17, 28). See also Hick, "Theology's Central Problem" (*GUF*, 2) and "Religion as Fact-Asserting," in *A John Hick Reader*, ed. Paul Badham (Philadelphia: Trinity Press International, 1990), 19, 30, 32.

[3] *PRP*, 46.

[4] Hick claims that the religions "are all, at their experiential roots, in contact with the same ultimate reality, but that their differing experiences of that reality, interacting over the centuries with the different thought-forms of different cultures have led to increasing differentiation and contrasting elaboration" (*GUF*, 146).

[5] See John Sanders, *No Other Name: An Investigation into the Destiny of the Unevangelized.* (Grand Rapids, MI: William B. Eerdmans Publishing Company, 1992), 119.

[6] An example of how the pluralistic hypothesis fosters reductionism is the circumstance that it gives no criterion for evaluating the *actual* truth-value of such contrary pairs of doctrine as the Hindu doctrine of ātman (there *is* an abiding self) or the Buddhist doctrine of anātman (there *is no* abiding self); the Hindu doctrine of avatāra, (incarnation, or divine descent), which places no limit in principle on how many incarnations there may be, or the Christian doctrine of incarnation, which limits incarnation to one person, one time, and one place; the Abrahamic doctrine of creation, which holds that the world is an arbitrary product of the divine will and is generated out of nonbeing, or the Greek and Indian doctrine of emanation, which holds that the world is an eternal process of lower grades of being emanating out of and returning to higher grades of being. In Hick's recent outlook, the truth or falsity of these doctrines is to be decided solely on the practical grounds of which is more likely to bring about a turn from self-centeredness to Reality-centeredness. Since all would, in Hick's estimation, be equally likely to

produce this effect, there is no *significant* difference to be found between these doctrines. Hick writes: "I have argued that each of the great traditions constitutes a context and, so far as human judgment can at present discern, a more or less equally effective context, for the transformation of human existence from self-centredness to Reality-centredness. Accordingly, *it does not seem to make any soteriological difference* whether one believes that the world is or is not eternal and its history cyclical or linear, that we do or do not reincarnate, that there are or are not angels and devils and a hierarchy of heavens and hells" (*IR*, 369, emphasis mine). This is a pragmatic reductionism, which is blind to the remaining theoretical issue of the *metaphysical* and *theological* truth of the particular doctrines in question. That question remains unanswered and insignificant from the standpoint of the pluralistic hypothesis.

[7] Kenneth Surin, "Towards a 'Materialist' Critique of 'Religious Pluralism': An Examination of the Discourse of John Hick and Wilfred Cantwell Smith," in *Religious Pluralism and Unbelief: Studies and Critical and Comparative*, ed. Ian Hammet (New York: Routledge 1990), 122.

[8] Surin, "Towards a 'Materialist Critique,'" 124.

[9] Ibid., 123.

[10] Ibid., 123. Surin elaborates on the notion of truth contained in this quote, a notion much influenced by Walter Benjamin. Surin writes: "In Benjamin's 'materialist' hermeneutic, the material content of an object originates at a specific, transient moment in history, and so the noumenal truth locked in objects can be released only when the historical truth contained in the concrete particular is released. And this truth is released only when the interpreter refrains from seeking to justify, to homogenize reality" (124).

[11] Ernst Troeltsch, "The Place of Christianity among the World Religions," (1923) reprinted in *Classical and Contemporary Readings in the Philosophy of Religion*, 3d ed., ed. John Hick (Englewood Cliffs, NJ: Prentice-Hall, 1990), 218.

[12] Troeltsch, "The Place of Christianity among the World Religions," 225.

[13] Thus, the pluralistic hypothesis and its soteriological criterion allow Hick to write that the various religions of the world "as vast complex totalities . . . seem to be more or less on a par with each other. None can be singled out as manifestly superior" ("The Non-Absoluteness of Christianity" [*MCU*, 30]).

[14] Bernard J. Verkamp agrees with this point: "Assuming, however, that all the religions deserve to be respected in their own right, the question still remains whether to show such respect it is necessary for Hick to go so far as to reject all their claims to uniqueness. . . . And is there not something ironic about religious pluralists asking us to respect all religions except for the one doctrine which they [the religions] almost all hold dear, namely, that in God's eyes they have been spe-

cially chosen to 'save' the rest of mankind? If, therefore, Hick's theory is ever to find acceptance among religious people themselves, it seems that he will leave greater room for the possibility that the various religions are, as Ernst Troeltsch notes, at least 'relatively absolute,' and interpret their claims to uniqueness perhaps as William Alston has done, in the sense, namely, that each religion represents the best and only path to salvation for its particular adherents in its own time and place" ("Hick's Interpretation of Religious Pluralism," *International Journal for Philosophy of Religion* 30 [1991]: 113).

[15] Since, on Hick's definition of the Real, no analogies between it and religious phenomena can be discovered by any process known to human beings, the noumenal Real can have no import for the philosophy of religions and no bearing on the issue of the cognitivity of religions.

[16] Newbigin discusses at some length the views of these writers in *The Gospel in a Pluralist Society* (Grand Rapids, MI: William B. Eerdmans Publishing Company, 1989), 155-70.

[17] Quoted in Harold Netland, *Dissonant Voices: Religious Pluralism and the Question of Truth* (Grand Rapids, MI: William B. Eerdmans Publishing Company), 34.

[18] Netland, *Dissonant Voices*, 34.

[19] In contrast to the weak exclusivist is what I call the *strong exclusivist*. The strong Christian exclusivist is inclined to see all religious activity outside Bible-believing fundamental churches as proceeding from Satan or demons. The strong exclusivist is inclined to see all other forms of religion as cultish and as demanding vigorous opposition by all legitimate means. Strong exclusivism motivated the following letter to the editor of *Christianity Today*, which is critical of an article published in that magazine entitled "The Hidden Gospel of the 12 Steps" [July 22, 1991]: "[This article] gives a solid example of how profit can be obtained at the forfeit of one's soul. In the raging battles of spiritual warfare, Satan can easily afford to exchange sobriety for a person's soul. Alcoholism is a crippling disease . . . but while [it] only destroy[s] the body, lack of faith in Jesus Christ brings the punishment of eternal destruction as well. Reformed alcoholics may fight the good fight and complete the course, but without keeping the faith in Jesus, the final prize is not theirs" [Paul Mega, *Christianity Today*, October 7, 1991]. This position finds theological expression in the writings of the conservative evangelical theologian Harold Lindsell, who asserts: "Regeneration is the real need of man. But man may not be regenerated either because he has not heard the Gospel without which regeneration is impossible or because he refused to avail himself of the benefits of the Gospel when he has heard it. Whichever it may be, the end is the same. He is permanently separated from God. Heaven and hell, then, are the competing options which unredeemed man faces" (quoted in Netland, *Dissonant Voices*, 265). Another conservative Christian scholar, Robert H. Gundry, asserts

that "the Bible is our only source of information concerning the status of the une-vangelized *heathen*. The notions of salvation through general revelation or after death find no solid footing in scripture. In fact the Bible indicates that apart from hearing and believing the Gospel the *heathen* are hopeless." (quoted in Netland, *Dissonant Voices*, 267, n. 80).

[20] Netland, *Dissonant Voices*,

[21] Ibid., 221–22.

[22] Ibid., 222.

[23] Ibid., 222.

[24] Ibid., 222.

[25] Other particularist Christian critiques of Hick's latest work include Gavin D'Costa, *Theology and Religious Pluralism: The Challenge of Other* Religions (Oxford: Basil Blackwell, 1986), Clark Pinnock, *A Wideness in God's Mercy: The Finality of Jesus Christ in a World of Religions* (Grand Rapids, MI: Zondervan Publishing House, 1992), John Sanders, *No other Name.: An Investigation into the Destiny of the Unevangelized.* (Grand Rapids, MI: William B. Eerdmans Publishing Company, 1992); Ronald H. Nash, *Is Jesus the Only Savior* (Grand Rapids, MI: Zondervan Publishing House, 1994), and Brad Stetson, *Pluralism and Particularity in Religious Belief* (Westport, CT: Praeger, 1994).

[26] The noumenal Real is also intended by Hick to serve as a constant reminder to the religious traditions that though they are concerned with the ultimately true and valuable, they have not yet nor can they ever attain a perfect clarity of in-sight, practice, and expression such that an exact correspondence of phenomenon and noumenon could be declared. That is, no religion is final, definitive, and abso-lute (P. Byrne makes a similar point when he writes with respect to Hick's plural-istic hypothesis: "by entertaining the thought of the thing-in-itself [i.e., the noumenal Real] we leave open the possibility that reality might have quite other properties than the ones our cognitive constitution allows us to perceive" ["A Religious Theory of Religion," *Scottish Journal of Theology* 35 (1982): 125]). How-ever, beyond this minimal function the doctrine of the noumenal Real could only be pushed if the Kantian critical ban on speculation and speech concerning transcen-dent realities like the Real were revoked.

[27] See also *PRP*, 106, where Hick writes that "we *postulate* that noumenon in af-firming the basic conviction that religious experience is not, as such, an illusory projection of our imaginations." See also Hick's Reply to Gavin D'Costa in Har-old Hewitt, Jr., ed. *Problems in the Philosophy of Religion: Critical Studies of the Work of John Hick* (New York: St. Martin's Press, 1991) 26.

[28] See also *IR* 134–35, 165, 169, 202, 244, 350.

[29] See also *IR*, 165, 350.

[30] What is implicit in this passage is explicit elsewhere: "the hypothesis of an ultimate divine noumenon is arrived at inductively" (*PRP*, 97). And "the pluralist hypothesis is arrived at inductively" (*PRP*, 37; see also 97, 103–4).

[31] Another way of putting this question is to ask whether the noumenal Real is only a human concept, providing the regulative functions of a transcendental postulate, but having no actual referent external to human languages, or whether the noumenal Real is also actually existent *in se* and not just a concept *pro nobis?* Michael Stoeber's critique of Hick's pluralistic hypothesis capitalizes on the inconsistency between Hick's "extreme constructivism" and his "position that the [noumenal] Real significantly impacts upon the mystic" ("Constructivist Epistemologies of Mysticism: A Critique and a Revision," *Religious Studies* 28 [March 1992]: 111). Stoeber links this ticklish position of Hick to the equally ticklish position of Kant, who, according to Stoeber, thinks that "the noumenon has some effect upon the experiencing subject even though the categories are in constant play" (110).

[32] It should be pointed out that such a defense would not be a *proof* of the truth of a religious interpretation of experience or that the divine reality plays a causal role in the generation of what religious people and religious interpreters of religion call religious experience. This stance, however, is in accord with Hick's rejection of the traditional and modern attempts to prove the existence of God. Rather than take such an approach Hick believes that, given certain conditions, it is *reasonable* for a religious person to trust her own personal experience. After the dismantling of the quasi-Kantian pluralistic hypothesis, the topic of trusting one's own religious experience (along with ancillary concepts), remains as the most promising strand in Hick's thought for developing a pluralistic hypothesis that can account for the plurality of religions as well as their cognitivity, their claim to veridicality.

[33] Keith Yandell's expression, quoted in *IR*, 239.

[34] Keith Ward, "Truth and the Diversity of Religions," *Religious Studies* 26 (1990): 6–9. See also Ward's *Religion and Revelation* (New York: Oxford University Press, 1994), 310–317.

[35] Ward, "Truth and the Diversity of Religions," 10.

[36] 1048B, trans. Rolt

[37] Ward, "Truth and Religious Diversity," 11; see also Gavin D'Costa, "John Hick and Religious Pluralism: Yet Another Revolution," in Hewitt, *Problems in the Philosophy of Religion*, 17, n. 26.

[38] Anthony O'Hear makes a similar criticism of Hick's unbalanced emphasis upon ineffability In "The real or the Real? Chardin or Rothko?" *Philosophy* 32 (1992): 55. O'Hear does not make use of the technical language of Thomas Aquinas or

Pseudo-Dionysius. Instead, he proposes an analogy between Hick's noumenal Real and the phenomenal religions and the abstract and indeterminate sublimity of a Rothko, which engulfs the perceiver and wipes away all determinations and horizons (50), and the aesthetic expressed in a Chardin, which "finds a real beauty in the midst of everyday domesticity" (48).

[39] Corroborating this conclusion is Peter Byrne's questioning "how far Hick's approach to living religions [in *An Interpretation of Religion*] genuinely captures the spirit of a realist attitude and makes any worthwhile use of the notion of truth in interpreting religion" ("A Religious Theory of Religion," *Religious Studies* 27 [1991]: 130).

[40] Gavin D'Costa thinks that Hick's recent views on religious pluralism undermine religious cognitivity and leads to what D'Costa characterizes as "transcendental agnosticism" (*John Hick's Theology of Religions: A Critical Evaluation* [Lanham, MD: University Press of America, 1987], 162, 167, 170). S. Mark Heim also criticizes Hick along these lines Hick: "If I were to say that I am a Christian and that in addition to being a Christian I also hold Hick's [pluralistic] hypothesis, what additional meaningful statement have I made? In terms of specifying or predicting a set of distinctive experiential circumstances, it seems I have made none. What the hypothesis does do is to commend a certain set of attitudes on my part and the part of others—attitudes of respect, humility, openness, which can be held also by those who do not affirm this hypothesis. It does exactly what non-realist accounts of religious language contend that language does. As such, *unconfused with a religious truth claim*, I can see no objection to it" ("The Pluralistic Hypothesis, Realism, and Post-Eschatology," *Religious Studies* 28 [1992]: 219 [emphasis mine]).

[41] Stephen Grover, "Unmatching Mysteries," review of *An Interpretation of Religion: Human Responses to the Transcendent*, by John Hick, *Times Literary Supplement*, 22–28 December 1989: 1404 (emphasis mine).

[42] Gerard Loughlin, "Prefacing Pluralism: John Hick and the Mastery of Religion," *Modern Theology* 7 (1990): 43. A similar point is made by Gavin D'Costa who writes about the "redundancy" noumenal Real in his essay in Hewitt, *Problems in the Philosophy of Religion*, 9.

[43] Kant's belief in the transcendental objectivity of the concepts of the understanding negates any notion of their cultural relativity, as at *Critique of Pure Reason*, A96.

[44] Compare *IR*, 242–45 with 343–47.

[45] That the view of cognitivity proposed in *An Interpretation of Religion* was developing even as Hick wrote this book is evidenced by lingering remnants of a literalist/propositionalist notion of cognitivity in the volume. For instance, Hick writes concerning conflicting doctrines that "although there must be true answers

to questions of this kind, we do not *know* the answers if 'we' here refers to humanity in general (369; see also 365). Yet, throughout most of *An Interpretation of Religion*, Hick has been developing the contrary position that discounts the cognitivity of the specific contents of doctrines, or the belief that there must be true answers to questions about conflicting doctrines and stories. Thus, he writes: "the truthfulness or untruthfulness of mythological stories, images, and conceptions does not consist in their literal adequacy to the nature of the Real *an sich*—in this respect it is not so much that they miss their target as that the target is totally beyond their range—but in their capacity to evoke appropriate or inappropriate dispositional responses to the Real" (353). Here, Hick asserts his developing view that cognitivity has nothing to do with specific truth-claims but rather with the power of stories and doctrines to orient us to something that is totally beyond their expressive power, whether figurative or literal. This view emerges, not without some backslidings, as the dominant view in *An Interpretation of Religion* (other passages that support the nullifying of the cognitive value of the content of specific doctrines and stories may be found at 278, 343, 347, 350, 352, 355–56, 359, 375, 371. There are also a lesser number of passages that seem to regress back to Hick's propositionalist view of cognitivity, such as those found at 173, 224, 363).

[46] Verkamp, "Hick's Interpretation of Religious Pluralism," 114, 123 n. 131.

[47] Heim criticizes Hick along just this line: "The challenge Hick has set himself is to provide a religious account of religion which is compatible with affirming an equal essential truth value and an identical soteriological result for all religions. What my analysis suggests is that the attempt to do this is, perhaps necessarily, required to be compatible with so many states of affairs that real cognitive content disappears. The various religious traditions, in running greater cognitive risk, escape at least this danger" ("The Pluralistic Hypothesis, Realism, and Post-Eschatology," 218).

[48] John Hick, *The Metaphor of God Incarnate: Christology in a Pluralistic* Age (Louisville, KY: Westminster/John Knox Press, 1993), 162–163.

Rethinking the Pluralistic Hypothesis

The aim of Hick's pluralistic hypothesis—the defense of the belief that religions are cognitive and that religious plurality does not threaten religious cognitivity—may be preserved without reductionism by purifying the notion of the Real of transcendental elements and by consistently portraying the Real as a *causal* factor in the generation of human religious experience.[1] The attempt to effect this purification will proceed by proposing a pluralistic hypothesis that dispenses with the conception of the Real as a transcendental postulate and begins anew with the claim that the Real is a partial transcendent cause of human religious experience. That is, religious experience does not spin itself out of only human elements, such as culture, psychology, biology, and the processes of the senses and the central nervous system. Given this view, it is possible to appropriate certain notions that run through all of Hick's writings, such as the cognitive ambiguity of the universe, human cognitive freedom, faith as interpretation, and the rationality of trusting one's experience. This complex of ideas is a dormant strand of assumptions in Hick's thought that is never deployed in meeting the challenge of religious pluralism, not even in *An Interpretation of Religion,* in which it might have proven most useful.

The Causes of the Diversity of Religious Experience

This alternative response to the problem of religious pluralism presupposes two basic elements. One is what Hick calls "the fact of finite freedom and the variety of forms which human life has taken in the ramifying exercise of this freedom" (*GHMNUS*, 111). The other is what he characterizes as "the openness of the Real to the traditions"(*IR*, 64). Implicit in these statements are two causal factors that figure in the production of religious experience. The first is the operation of diverse human personalities and cultures as filters through which the inexhaustible Real is refracted, thus offering resistance, in the electrical sense, over against the infinite Real. The second is the revelatory openness of the Real to a potential infinity of finite traditions, cultures, and persons. Exploring the ramifications of these lines of thought will help to determine whether Hick's own thought contains an alternative to the present version of the pluralistic hypothesis, an alternative that can uphold religious cognitivity without succumbing to reductionism or an empty transcendentalism.

Filters and Resistance: Persons and Cultures as Partial Causes of Religious Experience

Hick speculates that religious experience is, in part, a product of "the impact of transcendent reality" upon the one having this kind of experience (*IR*, 165). This view is consistent with his conviction, or faith, that the Real environs the totality of physical existence (*IR*, 163). Because, human beings, being finite, have a limited capacity for direct encounter with the Real, Hick suggests that individual human beings are protected from an overwhelmingly direct encounter with the Real by a system of filtration through which the Real is reduced to forms with which finite beings can cope.[2]

This need for filtration occurs not only in relation to the infinite Real but also with respect to the deceptively ordinary objects of everyday experience. Hick suggests that the senses and nervous system prevent the experience of drinking a glass of water from taking on the aspect of a psychedelic experience:

> If . . . instead of seeing water as the continuous shiny substance that we can drink we perceived it as a cloud of electrons in rapid swirling motion, and the glass that holds it as a mass of brilliantly coloured crystals, themselves composed of particles in violent activity, then drinking a glass of water, instead of being routine, would be a startling adventure (*IR*, 135).[3]

This exposure to an excess of reality would prove a tremendous distraction and require an exhausting expenditure of energy to endure if it were a continuous experience. However, the senses and nervous system construct a simplified version of the world in which we can live successfully and with a minimum of distraction (*IR*, 136).

In Hick's view, religions function as filters in the same way. He claims that

> the human mind [is] protected from an overwhelmingly direct presence of the Real by religion itself, functioning as a system for filtering out the infinite divine reality and reducing it to [manageable] forms. . . . The effect of the different 'sacred canopies' has been to enable us to be touched by the Real, and yet only partially and selectively, in step with our own spiritual development, both communal and individual (*IR*, 163).

That is, religions are filters embodying a complex of functions, concepts, activities, and mythical entities, personal and impersonal, that bring us into contact with the Real while protecting us from it at the same time.[4] Were we to confront the Real without the aid of the filtering devices of religion, culture, senses, and the nervous system, we would have an encounter far more devastating and awesome than that with a mere glass of water. For to perceive in all of its awesome depth the "total claim" that the infinite Real, as our origin, norm, and end, makes upon us would be to reduce us to nothing and deprive us of our relative freedom and personhood.[5] As a filtering device, religion makes possible a limited but genuine and free encounter with the sacred.

Hick builds upon the metaphor of filter by introducing the metaphor of resistance. In his view, religion, by refracting the Real through various systems of filters, functions as our "resistance (in a sense analogous to the use of the word in electronics) to the Real" (*IR*, 163). Although both of these concepts—filtration and resistance—seem crude and too technological to be useful in explicating religion, they are nonetheless helpful. The notion of religions as filters is straightforward enough. The notion of religion as analogous to electrical resistance becomes clearer when one explores the concept of electrical resistance. Simply stated, electrical resistance is the reciprocal of electrical conductivity. That is, resistance can be defined as "a property of an electric circuit or part of a circuit that transforms electric energy into heat energy in opposing electric current."[6] Electrical resistance is caused by collisions between a current of electrically charged particles and the fixed particles of the structure of the metal or other substance that conduct the electrical current. Thus, except for certain conductors that have zero resistance when supercooled, all conductors have some degree of resistance. Electrical engineers use resistors, which are electrical components that control the degree of conductivity of an electrical current through a circuit, in order to shape the current to suit a certain purpose. For example, the brightness of an electric light can be controlled by the use of an adjustable resistor, or a rheostat, which varies the amount of current in the circuit by adjusting the degree of resistance.

By analogy, religions, cultures, and the body's sensory and neural processes can be seen as adjustable resistors, or rheostats, which serve to control the current of the Real conducted by the individual human being or culture. Just as an electrical engineer can manipulate resistance to create circuits of different shapes, thus causally interacting with electrical current to design a variety of electrical devices, such as rheostatically controlled lamps, electronic circuit boards, and computer chips, so religions, cultures, and the body's sensory and neural processes are resistors that causally interact with the current of the infinite Real and shape various apprehensions of the Real that are suited to the various temperaments of diverse human beings and cultures. In short, religions (along with cultures and sensory and neural processes) are partial causes of the various shapes or patterns of the varieties of religious experience afforded by the many religious traditions.

Revelatory Openness: The Infinite Real as Partial Cause of Religious Experience

Alongside the human causes of religious experience, Hick is convinced that the Real is also a partial but essential cause of such experience.[7] For Hick, the Real as a cause intersects with the human causes (i.e., religions, cultures, biology, and personality), thereby creating religious experience. In Hick's view, religious experience in all its varieties "arises at the interface between the Real and the human spirit, and is thus a joint product of transcendent presence and earthly imagination, of divine revelation and human seeking" (*IR*, 266).

Hick refers to the nonhuman side of this causal nexus as "informational input from external reality," an "impact . . . generating information that is transformed into a conscious mode," or "the impact of transcendent reality."[8] In Hick's view, the affectional Real is only a *partial* cause of religious experience.[9] Its action upon a human being allows the person who freely responds to it to bring a distinctive contribution to a whole that we call religious experience. These human contributions are products of the specific personalities, cultures, and sensory and neurological capacities of the various individuals who choose to respond affirmatively to the impact of the Real. The rich diversity of religious life flows out of this mutual activity of the human beings and the Real.

The causes of religious diversity, then, are to be found in the diversity of the two contributing causes, the human and the Real, that constitute it. Maintaining that both poles (the human and the Real) in combination are the causes of religious experience is what distinguishes a religious from a nonreligious, noncognitive, or merely functionalist interpretation of religious experience. The latter sorts of interpretation are concerned merely with the human causes of such experience and do not, from Hick's standpoint, exhaust the possibilities of interpreting that experience. There is no need, however, to resort to the ultimately futile complications of the quasi-Kantian version of the pluralistic hypothesis. Hick already has sufficient resources to address the issue of religious pluralism and relativism in his doctrine of the dual causation of religious experience, which arises at the interface of the human and the Real.

This approach is non-Kantian. It presupposes no noumenon/phenomenon distinction or dichotomy. Consequently, it does not deny the possibility of increasing speculative and empirical knowledge of the causal role of the transcendent (not transcendental) Real in the production of human experience. However, given the finitude of human knowledge, one must always speak modestly and tentatively about a reality whose existence seems warranted by the experiences of particular individuals and communities. The ineffability of the Real is not a *critical* ineffability, which bars *in principle* any knowledge of transcendent reality because of a supposed epistemic and metaphysical dichotomy between human experience and that which transcends human experience (indeed, claiming that there is such a dichotomy is self-defeating, since such a claim is metaphysical and thus violates the limitations asserted by a critical epistemology). On the contrary, the Real is partially ineffable. That is, there is no formal dichotomy between human experience and that which transcends it. For how could we, as finite beings, say where a supposed line between the finite and the infinite should be drawn? Surely that would involve a large dose of metaphysical hubris. Rather there is only the fluid distinction between the degree of reality that a finite organism can apprehend and the whole of reality itself, which transcends the capacities of all organisms, potential and actual. One can always move more deeply into that transcendent dimension of the Real, though one can never exhaust it. If one conceives the Real as simply the element of transcendence in human experience, then, in principle, there is no reason why one may not speculate about it by way of the usual analogical, metaphorical, and mythological means.

By connecting these causal presuppositions to other notions that have been central to Hick's thinking since the beginning of his career—the cognitive ambiguity of the universe, human cognitive freedom, faith as interpretation, and the rationality of trusting one's experience—it should become clear that there are resources within Hick's writings that allow for a nontranscendental pluralistic hypothesis, one that avoids the reductionism and inutility characteristic of his quasi-Kantian notion of the Real *an sich*.

Elements of a Nontranscendental Pluralistic Hypothesis

The Cognitive Ambiguity of the Universe

One of the central contentions of John Hick's work in the philosophy of religion is that "the theistic and the anti-theistic arguments are all inconclusive" (*IR*, 12). Hick has come to this conclusion after much thought and writing about the traditional and modern arguments for the existence of God (*IR*, 73–125). He holds this view because, as he writes: "the special evidences to which [the various arguments] appeal are also capable of being understood in terms of the contrary world-view" (*IR*, 12).

Although the failure of these arguments has not persuaded Hick to surrender his conviction that religions emerge from human encounters with the Real, the inadequacy of the arguments has led him to conclude that the universe as it confronts human beings is religiously ambiguous (*PRP*, 110). That is, we can interpret it either religiously or "naturalistically" (i.e., noncognitively, nonreligiously, or merely functionally).[10] Hick writes:

> The world in which we find ourselves is religiously ambiguous. It is possible for different people (as also for the same person at different times) to experience it both religiously and nonreligiously; and to hold beliefs which arise from and feed into each of these ways of experiencing (*PRP*, 110).

Because of this ambiguity we are unable to determine *absolutely* which of the various religious and nonreligious interpretations of the universe is the most adequate, though individual and communal experience may persuade one of the truth of one or another of these various interpretations. Nevertheless, we cannot force any favored interpretation onto the universe and demand universal allegiance to it without overlooking the simple truth that no sure method has been found that will give final, unimpeachable authority to any of the many available interpretations of the universe. According to Hick, therefore, the religious ambiguity of the universe must simply be accepted as a pervasive and irresolvable condition of human experience (*PRP*, 27).

One should not assume at this point that Hick has succumbed to relativism or irrealism—a great temptation for philosophers who have been reared in but have outgrown positivistic ways of thinking. There are resources within Hick's writings that help him to avoid the religious relativism that the notion of cognitive ambiguity seems to imply. In Hick's view, the criterion for the truthfulness of a religious doctrine or story is the soteriological criterion. That is, the truth of a religious doctrine or story is determined by asking whether or not it conduces to saintliness, or the overcoming of selfishness in favor of service to others and the Real. Given this criterion, Hick can judge between better and worse religious views. He can determine, for instance, that a religious view that prescribes human or animal sacrifice is a worse viewpoint than one that proscribes such activities. The ambiguity of the world is, thus, not total, since Hick thinks that the truth of various religious hypotheses is related to their power to facilitate selflessness and the service of others and the Real. By making the connection between the truth of religious hypotheses and the soteriological criterion, Hick provides a realist way of mitigating to a great degree the ambiguity that attends cosmic hypotheses.

Human Cognitive Freedom

Cognitive ambiguity dilutes the totalizing impulse of religious hypotheses about the character of the universe and works similarly upon the totalizing impulse of nonreligious interpretations of the world as well. However, a thoroughgoing metaphysical and theological skepticism is not warranted by this insight into the limits of cosmic hypotheses. Ambiguity is not negation. The world is ambiguous because different people using different models, hypotheses, or frames of reference for interpreting the universe have varying degrees of success.[11] The same bit of evidence—the death of a loved one, a natural calamity, or an illness, for example—may serve the very different purposes of the theist who sees in them "the hand of God" and the atheist who sees in them the negation of the claim that a powerful, loving, and wise God exists. It is unlikely that the theist and the atheist could ever come to agreement, because they look at the same events through the lenses of irreconcilable speculative models of reality. The sources of these models are not entirely rational, but include emotional, familial, cultural, and dispositional factors. As Hick observes:

> We have a dual capacity to allow the Real to become present to us as the all-transforming reality or to shut it out of our consciousness. . . . in so far as we are in our deepest dispositional nature open and responsive to the Real, we can receive an authentic awareness of it in one (or more) of its manifestations (*IR*, 162).

In this analysis, a religious response to the Real is ever present as a potential dimension of human experience, although it is not one that will ever be universally shared by all people. Making a virtue out of necessity, Hick sees providence at work in the cognitive ambiguity of the world and its resistance to totalizing hypotheses (Hick would likely also include relativism among such totalizing hypotheses). In Hick's view, this ambiguity allows human beings a wide latitude of cognitive freedom with respect to beliefs about the religious or nonreligious character of the ultimately real. This cognitive freedom is designed, in Hick's view, to protect our freedom and autonomy from being overwhelmed by the infinity of the Real and its demand that we transcend our finite and self-centered aims and conform to infinitely high and inexhaustible ethical demands. Hick argues that

> this cognitive freedom in relation to the Real also has a negative function, namely to protect our finite freedom and autonomy. For to be a particular kind of creature is to be structured to cognise and participate in reality in a particular way; and for a creature to have imposed upon it a more extensive or intensive awareness than it is able to assimilate, compulsorily revealing to it a more complex or value-laden environment than it can respond to, would be destructive (*IR*, 162).

A naked encounter with the infinite Real would be lopsidedly unfair to and coercive of human beings, thus depriving us of free will, and would threaten to overwhelm our finite minds, thereby deranging and dissolving them. In illustration of this point, Hick quotes T. S. Eliot: "human kind/Cannot bear very much reality."[12] One may equally well quote Emily Dickinson: "The Truth must dazzle gradually/Or every man be blind."[13] To prevent this uneven engagement, the Real presents itself as a "non-coercive presence" (*WBG*, 67). This noncoerciveness is accomplished by the veiling of the Real under the diverse images and models suggested by the world's religious traditions, whose truth, in Hick's view, can be determined only by their faithfulness to the soteriological criterion of producing saintliness.

Faith as Interpretation

Another notion in Hick's writings that may be used to counter the quasi Kantianism of the pluralistic hypothesis, is that of faith as "the element of uncompelled interpretation within the experience of divine presence" (or what Hick now calls *the Real*) (*FK2*, ix).[14] Faith, or uncompelled interpretation, is the connection between the infinite Real and finite human beings that preserves human freedom and individual integrity while allowing a mode of relationship with the Real for those who are open to it. Hick explains that "it is the interpretive element within religious experience [i.e., faith] that enables us to enter into an uncompelled, though always necessarily limited and mediated, awareness of the Real" (*IR*, 162).

Faith as interpretation, along with cognitive freedom and cognitive ambiguity, are ingredients in the act of understanding. This includes the freedom to reject religious faith, or a religious interpretation of reality. Faith, then, can be defined as a particular kind of interpretative act, namely an exercise of our cognitive freedom in favor of religious hypotheses.[15]

Hick discounts the possibility that there can ever be a direct, uninterpreted encounter with the Real, either in this life or in another, should there be one, for "heavenly cognition, like earthly cognition, will still involve the element of interpretation, which for one I wish to identify with faith" (*PRP*, 119). Thus, faith is an interpretation of experience of no less worth than other kinds of "faith," such as nonreligious interpretations of the world. He writes:

> Both the religious and the naturalistic ways of construing the world arise from a fundamental cognitive choice, which I call faith, which is continuous with the interpretive element within our experience of the physical and ethical character of our environment (*IR*, 13).

The Rationality of Trusting One's Experience

The ideas of cognitive freedom, cognitive ambiguity, and faith as a mode of interpretation reflect Hick's enduring central belief that

> it is rationally appropriate for those who experience their life in relation to the transcendent to trust their own experience, together with that of the stream of religious life in which they participate and of the great figures who are its primary experiential witnesses, and to proceed to live and to believe on that basis (*IR*, 13).

Hick believes that because we operate on what Richard Swinburne calls the *principle of credulity*, it is normal for us to "live on the basis of trust in the veridical character of our experience" (*IR*, 214). For "unless we trust our own experience we can have no reason to believe anything about the nature, or indeed the existence, of the universe in which we find ourselves" (*IR*, 216).

Consequently, Hick thinks a person who has been experientially gripped by the Real has a cognitive right or perhaps even an obligation to act in accordance with this experience. Hick writes:

> what we designate as sanity consists in acting on the basis of our putatively cognitive experience as a whole. We cannot go beyond that; for there is no "beyond" to go to, since any further datum of which we may

become aware will then form part of our total experience. And if some aspect of it is sufficiently intrusive or persistent, and generally coherent with the rest, to reject it would amount to a kind of cognitive suicide. One who has a powerful and continuous sense of existing in the presence of God *ought* therefore to be convinced that God exists. Accordingly the religious person, experiencing life in terms of the divine presence, is rationally entitled to believe what he or she experiences to be the case—namely that God is real, or exists (*IR*, 216).

Although Hick thinks that human beings are rational in acting in accordance with what is true to their experience, he has always been quick to point out that one may be wrong in trusting one's experience, since one has no way of stepping outside of one's experience to see whether or not the experience is delusory.[16] After all not only saintly religious persons, but also religious terrorists are paradigmatic instances of persons living on the basis of trust in the veridical character of their experience. Proponents of apartheid, segregation, slavery, and anti-Semitism have found grounds in their religious traditions that make it seem rational to them to uphold these viewpoints.

However, that Hick cannot be charged with holding a viewpoint that would be so promiscuous as to grant the status of reasonableness to the viewpoints mentioned, even if sanctioned by an internally coherent religious viewpoint. The reason for this is that Hick holds religious traditions to the standard of producing saints, i.e., increasing the number of those who serve others and the Real at the expense of their self-regarding egos.

This approach, though staving off relativism, pays a high price. Reliance on the soteriological criterion as a means of determining what is true doctrine is reductionistic, since in practice it dispenses with the issue of the truth of diverse religious doctrines and stories by asserting that a doctrine or story is true only insofar as it is conducive to the production of saintliness. Thus, the various aspects of religious doctrines and stories that do not have directly to do with the production of saints are reduced to secondary importance.

Doctrinal Fidelity and Religious Tolerance

The issue, then, that must be faced if my reconstruction of Hick's pluralistic hypothesis in terms of the complex of notions explicated above is to be plausible is this: how to keep in view at the same time the ever elusive question of the truth of particular religious doctrines and stories and also the never dispensable requirement that what one believes not break the bonds of a tolerance that is grounded in respect for all other human beings? Such an approach would be able to make moral judgments about those religious views that demean other human beings while keeping open such strictly doctrinal questions, which remain unsettled but of great significance, such as whether *ātman* or *anātman* is true, whether Jesus is the ultimate revelation, or whether one may discover independent and saving revelation in the scriptures of other traditions, ancient and modern.

To achieve this balancing of the question of the truth of particular doctrines and stories and a tolerance grounded in respect for all human beings requires the rejection of Hick's arbitrary belief that the various religious traditions are more or less equal in their salvific capacity. Hick writes that

> if we now attempt comparative judgments, asking whether tradition A has produced more, or better, saints per million of population than tradition B, we quickly discover that we do not have sufficient information for an answer. All that I myself feel able to venture at present is the impressionistic judgment that no one tradition stands out as more productive of sainthood than another. I suggest that so far as we can tell they constitute to about the same extent contexts within which the transformation of human existence from self-centredness to Reality-centredness is taking place. The criterion of saintliness [that is, the soteriological criterion], then, enables us to recognise the great traditions as areas of salva-

tion/liberation, but does not enable us to go on and grade them comparatively (*IR*, 307).

There is no compelling reason to credit this belief, even if, for reasons of civility, we cannot or do not wish to say *which* of the traditions is relatively more or less salvific, enlightening, or humanizing. Civility aside, one may just as easily say that *all of the traditions are equally damnable, unenlightened, and dehumanizing.* Religions often cast a frightful mien upon many who differ from what they teach or who oppose them. Examples abound. The threat to individual freedoms, especially those of women, and the promise of the restoration of cruel and unusual forms of punishment posed by the rise of Islāmic fundamentalism in Algeria in early 1992; the bloody and continuing strife between Muslims and Hindu fundamentalists at the site of a Muslim *masjid* built at the mythological birthplace of Rāma in Ayodhya; the long struggle between Christian and Muslim Arab militias in Lebanon; the continuing struggle between Muslim terrorists and ultra-orthodox Jewish settlers on the West Bank in Palestine; the long, bloody, and futile battle between Roman Catholic extremists and Protestant fundamentalists in Northern Ireland; the unspeakably bloody struggle between Hindu Tamils and Buddhist Sinhalese in Sri Lanka, a struggle that claimed the life of Rajiv Gandhi; the cruel conflict between Hindus and Sikhs in the Punjab, a conflict that claimed the life of Rajiv's Mother, Indira Gandhi—this turbulence in the realm of religion understandably moves many observers to reject religion as irrational and to deny it any role in the public life of nations, as has been more or less achieved, though always tenuously, in the United States through the establishment clause in the First Amendment. A charitable observer, noting certain inspiring religious *individuals,* such as Martin Luther King, Malcolm X (after his pilgrimage to Mecca), Mother Teresa, Mahatma Gandhi, and other notable figures may allow that on rare occasions a person of saintly proclivities rises above the strife of religions as *collectivities* and articulates a nobler religious vision of reality, one which demands wisdom, compassion, and tolerance, and which refuses to countenance the self-righteousness and fanaticism of those who are blinded and corrupted by religious differences made absolute.

How can this bleak and irrational strife of religious absolutisms and exclusivisms be overcome in such a way that the genius of religions in producing saints may be accomplished without demanding of the religions that they pare away central doctrines that are not reducible to the dimensions of the soteriological criterion but, that, nevertheless, do not conflict with a universal, non-relativistic tolerance grounded in respect? An answer may be found in the notion of a universal conversation among religionists, which is grounded in a non-negotiable respect for human dignity and a respect for the traditional teachings of each religion.

Truth and Conversation

If truth is an emergent feature of the conversation of human beings of any and all tribes and races and creeds talking earnestly with one another; if truth emerges from the passionate, sometimes disagreeable and contentious, but never abandoned conversation between physicists, philosophers, religionists, mystics, humanists, atheists, jurists, French poststructuralists, nontranscendentalist Thomists, Hindus, post-Marxists, feminists, and the proverbial average man and woman on the street, then there is always the possibility that there will be real gains in understanding among them, especially when the temptation to end the conversation is at its strongest. In this promiscuous and universal conversation, everyone must abandon the attempt to corner the market metaphysically or epistemologically or, failing that, falling into a sulk while declaiming that all this talk isn't worth the candle. In this way, the narrow and tortuous path between dogmatism and skepticism, between reductionism and relativism, may cautiously be negotiated. As Hilary Putnam writes: "Perhaps we can come to see criticism as a conversation with many voices rather than as a contest with winners and losers."[17] Or as Gordon Kaufman writes:

> Free-flowing conversation presupposes a consciousness of being but one participant in a larger, developing yet open-ended, pattern of many voices, each having its own integrity, none being reducible to any of the others; and it presupposes a willingness to be but one voice in this developing texture of words and ideas, with no desire to control the entire movement (as in a lecture or a monologue). When theological or religious truth is conceived in these pluralistic and dialogical terms, no single voice can lay claim to it, for each understands that only in the ongoing conversation as a whole is truth brought into being. In this model truth is never final or complete or unchanging: it develops and is transformed in unpredictable ways as the conversation proceeds.[18]

Seeing truth as an emergent characteristic of continuing conversation also confers a further benefit upon those who stick with it: the exorcism of the overrated hobgoblin of relativism. This claim can be illuminated with an analogy, or rather a disanalogy. A standard ploy of relativists (who seem in many instances to be frustrated absolutists and exclusivists) is to claim, for example, that an implication of the change in the view of the earth as flat to the view that the earth is round is that truth is mutable, a creature that is entirely a product of diverse times and places and as diverse as those spatiotemporal locations. Thus, by analogy, any so-called truth of which we are now persuaded may and probably will in time be replaced by a new truth more palatable to the interests of future times and other places.

However, this analogy does not hold; actually it is a disanalogy. It implies that we stand in the same relation to our *present* beliefs as we do to old, discarded, or reformed beliefs. Yet this is simply not the case. For we can survey the stream of beliefs that have emerged in the history of human conversation and point out those that have been replaced or improved upon by other beliefs, but we cannot *now* point out which of our *current* beliefs will turn out to be either false or inadequate in the future. Some of our certainties will become uncertainties, and some of our uncertainties will become certainties, while whole new realms of thoughts will emerge almost magically from now unthinkable depths and corners of the mystery of our existence. As Wittgenstein wrote: "The river-bed of thoughts may shift."[19] Thus, the course of the emergence of future beliefs in the ever-widening conversation of humankind cannot be predicted, but, so long as humankind survives and continues to expand the circle of conversation, these beliefs will emerge as we talk and argue, defend and concede, offer reasons, and tell stories.

This universal conversation must be a human imperative in the present and future on a planet that can increasingly ill afford violence to proceed from religious, ideological, ethnic, and linguistic differences. Thus, we, as finite human knowers, must all abandon the notion that surfaces in numerous disguises throughout the history of Western philosophy that knowledge is *epistēmē*. In its place we must affirm that for us—if not for angels and gods, if such intelligences there be—knowledge is always *doxa*. To deny this is an instance of a philosophical hubris whose sure penalty is contempt for philosophy itself, that instinctual asking of the deep questions of life, which unbidden and irrepressibly proceeds from within the mystery of our individual existence. To scorn this questioning is to scorn being human, a vice that replicates, in its results at least, the scorn of mere humanness that inspires absolutism and exclusivism in the first place. Leaving behind these twin vices, so destructive of our humanity, we ought to follow the advice of Wittgenstein, who urged: *"Laß uns menschlich sein."*[20]

Notes

[1] Whether or not one would agree with Hick that the Real can be a causal factor in the generation of religious experience, one can make Hick's thought consistent in this area only by emphasizing the Real as an actual causal rather than a merely formal transcendental entity.

[2] The notion, or metaphor, of a filter is derived by Hick from Henri Bergson, who, in Hick's words, claimed that "one function of the brain is to filter out the virtual infinity of information reaching us through our senses, so that what comes to consciousness is the relatively simple and manageable world we perceive and can successfully inhabit" (John Hick, "Mystical Experience as Cognition," in *Understanding Mysticism*, ed. Richard Woods [Garden City, NY: Doubleday & Company, 1980], 432).

[3] See also *GHMNUS*, 112.

[4] Hick writes: "It is important to remember that religious traditions, considered as 'filters' . . . function as totalities which include not only concepts and images of God [or the Real], with the modes of religious experience which they inform, but also systems of doctrine, ritual, and myth, and art forms, moral codes, life-styles, and often patterns of social organization" (Hick, *GHMNUS*, 113).

[5] Hick claims that "in relation to that which has absolute reality and value, I am nothing and can have no personal being and freedom in relation to it unless the infinitely valuable reality permits me largely to shut it out of my consciousness. Thus we preserve our freedom over against the infinite reality which, as absolute value, makes a total claim upon us, by being aware of it in terms of limited and limiting concepts and images" (*GHMNUS*, 111).

[6] This quote and the information in this paragraph are derived from *Encyclopedia Brittanica*, 15th ed. (1990), s.v. "resistance," "resistivity," "resistor."

[7] Hick offers no proof for this speculative, metaphysical belief other than that of his own experience and his recognition of what he believes are traces of the causal influence of the Real in the descriptions of religious experience offered by other traditions.

[8] *IR*, 243, 167, 165. Hick could make a relative distinction between human and transhuman experience (the latter being that which affects human receptivity) simply by pointing out that there is always an element of inexplicable transcendence in human experience.

[9] "All that we are entitled to say about the noumenal source of this information is that it is the reality whose influence produces, *in collaboration with the human*

mind, the phenomenal world of our experience" (*IR,* 243, emphasis mine). Here Hick is caught in a contradiction, necessitated by his quasi-Kantian stricture on speech about the noumenal Real. One rightly asks how Hick, given this stricture, can be "entitled" to say even this much about the supposedly unknowable Real.

[10] The inaccuracy of Hick's use of the term *naturalistic* to stand for noncognitive, nonreligious, and merely functional interpretations of religion was discussed in chapter two.

[11] This is not a relativistic position, because "success" in these instances would be judged by Hick by means of the soteriological criterion, as discussed above and in chapter three.

[12] *Four Quartets,* "Burnt Norton," sec. 1, lines 44–45; quoted in Hick, *IR,* 162.

[13] "Tell All the Truth," lines 7–8. Jaroslav Pelikan, writing of the theology of the Fathers of Eastern Christendom, in particular that of the apophatic theologians Pseudo-Dionysius and Maximus the Confessor, writes, relevantly to the point at hand, that "the true knowledge of God in himself would have to be as unmeasured as God. If God, who was literally 'immense [*ametrētos*]' (that is, not large, but beyond measure), were to reveal himself in his true being, the trauma to the human mind would be the same as that inflicted by the unveiled sun on the naked eye" (*The Spirit of Eastern Christendom (600–1700)* [Chicago: University of Chicago Press, 1974], 32).

[14] Should one ask what Hick means by the term *divine,* I would answer that he uses this term to refer to the dimension of transcendence that is an essential element of all human experience. He writes that "the environment in which we are conscious of living always transcends the physical impacts of the world upon our sense organs. Accordingly we cannot avoid the idea of the transcendent: for meaning is always couched partly in terms that exceed the immediately given" (*IR,* 136).

[15] Hick defines faith in these terms: "Religious faith then, as I propose to use the term, is that uncompelled subjective contribution to conscious experience which is responsible for its distinctively religious character" (*IR,* 160).

[16] Throughout his writings, Hick acknowledges the lack of objective certainty that attends even one's most commonplace and experientially valid beliefs. Thus he warns that "the highest degree of 'self-evidence,' the most intense feelings of self-authenticating insight, can be utterly delusive" (*FK1,* 16). He emphatically denies that one person's account of her religious experience provides an adequate reason for a person who doubts the reality of such an experience to accept the existence of the Real or that the existence of God can be inferred from reports of religious experience (*FK2,* 209). Consistently with this position, Hick thinks that for "a theology without proofs the central epistemological problem becomes that of the nature of faith" (*FK1,* xvii). Hick includes the so-called argument from religious experience in his negative evaluation of the theistic proofs, because he recognizes

the fallibility of all cognition, knowledge, and experience. Hick writes that when we come to "the sixty-four thousand dollar question of the validity or trustworthiness of religious experience. . . . [it must be said] that such experiences do not *prove* the existence of God" (Hick, *WBF*, 43). Religious knowledge or experience is no more exempt from this limitation upon human knowledge than is scientific or any other variety of knowing. As Hick admits that "we still cannot be happy to say that *all* religious and quasi-religious experiences without exception provide a good grounding for beliefs. There are errors and delusions in other spheres and we must expect there to be such in religion also" (Hick, *IR*, 217). Hick also writes that "[a]ll our cognitions are fallible" (Hick, *FK1*, 12). Once these cautionary statements are taken into account, there still remains to the religious person a basic right to trust as veridical her experiences of the presence of the Real, unless persuasive evidence to the contrary becomes available.

[17] Hilary Putnam, *Realism with a Human Face*. (Cambridge: Harvard University Press, 1990), 213. The larger context within which this sentence occurs is: "If new exegeses and new critical interpretations are always necessary, if there is no convergence to One True Interpretation, then, by the same token, the fashion of seeing the interpretations of past centuries as *wholly* superseded by contemporary 'insights' may be recognized as the naive progressivism that it is. Perhaps we can come to see criticism as a conversation with many voices rather than as a contest with winners and losers." The paragraph from which this sentence comes can be applied just as well to the diversity or religious interpretations as to the interpretation of fiction, the topic with which Putnam is concerned in the article from which the quote comes, "Is There a Fact of the Matter about Fiction?"

[18] Kaufman, "Mystery, Theology, and Conversation," *Harvard Divinity Bulletin* 21 (1991-92): 13.

[19] Ludwig Wittgenstein, *On Certainty*, §97; quoted in Charles Guignon, "Philosophy after Wittgenstein and Heidegger," *Philosophy and Phenomenological Research* 50 (1990): 667.

[20] Ludwig Wittgenstein, *Vermischte Bemerkungen*, 30; quoted in Joseph M. Incandela, "The Appropriation of Wittgenstein's Work by Philosophers of Religion: Towards a Re-evaluation and an End," *Religious Studies* 21 (1985): 466.

Appendix

The Principle of Cognitive Equivalence

The apparent ease with which the verification principle in its earliest, most stringent, version was able to negate the cognitivity of metaphysics and theology was due to its dependence upon operational definitions, in which scientific concepts are defined in terms of operations that produce some observable result.[1] "Current is flowing in the wire if and only if the voltmeter needle is deflected" is an operational definition. In accordance with the most stringent version of the verification principle, the two statements in this biconditional proposition are thought to be cognitively equivalent because they must have the same testable consequences.[2] That is, these two statements are equivalent in meaning: when current flows in the wire, the needle of the voltmeter is deflected, and vice versa. This way of defining *current* depends not on theories about electricity, but only on the results of certain operations—in the case, the consulting of a voltmeter. Thus any meaning attributed to the word *current* beyond that given in the right side of the equivalence statement ("the voltmeter needle is deflected"[3]) would have to be rejected as a spurious "transcendental meaning,"[4] having no cognitive value within the positivistic view of scientific method.

Hans Reichenbach, one of the leading logical empiricists, showed how the principle of equivalence can be used to disembowel metaphysics and theology.[5] Consider the case of the cat worshippers, as recounted by Hilary Putnam:

> Reichenbach imagines a group of cat worshippers. These people maintain the sentence *Cats are divine animals*. When asked what signs there are

that this is true, or what testable consequences their belief has, they point to the fact that cats produce a state of awe (in cat worshippers).[6]

Reichenbach sees this as a case of cognitive equivalence. That is, the theological claim about cats is meaningful if and only if the psychological claim about the mental states of cat-worshippers is meaningful. Whatever residue of meaning the theological statement ("Cats are divine animals") contains over and above the psychological claim must be rejected as a spurious transcendental meaning, or, more pejoratively, as metaphysical nonsense.

In this case, Reichenbach thinks like a vulgar positivist, although his analysis of equivalence was actually conceived in opposition to just this crude use of equivalence in early verificationism. According to Putnam, Reichenbach did *"not* intend it to turn out that any two theories with the same *testable consequences* must turn out to be equivalent descriptions."[7] More consistent with this intention was Reichenbach's case of the cubical world, which, following Putnam, can be stated as follows. Shadows cast by objects upon the large translucent cube that encloses the cubical world within which all intelligent observers live are the only signals from the outside world that can be seen within the cubical world. Scientists inside the cube, noticing the similarity of certain exactly described shadows cast from outside the cube to the shadows made by birds within the cube, infer on the basis of these shadows that there are birds outside of the cube. This claim instigates a dispute between positivists and realists. The positivists claim that talk about birds outside the cube is derivative from talk about the shadows on the walls, since talk about birds on the outside can be verified when and only when shadows appear on the walls of the cube. The realists claim that talk about birds on the outside is not derivative from talk about shadows, since birds are one thing and shadows another.[8]

Reichenbach allies himself with the realists in this dispute,[9] because he thinks that the statement about birds and the statement about shadows have a different degree of probability, *even though* they have the same testable consequences. That is, whether birds outside the cube cause the shadows or not, the results are the same. However, this identity of testable consequences does not validate the positivist claim that talk about the shadows as derivative from knowledge of birds within the cube is cognitively equivalent to talk about actual birds outside the cube which are thought to cause the shadows. The positivists are correct with respect to the identity of testable consequences, but this does not decide the issue between the realists and the positivists with regard to the cognitive equivalence of these very different ways of accounting for the bird-like shadows on the walls of the cubical world. This is because the probability of verifying these ways of talking are different. Given that the inhabitants of the cubical world have never actually seen the postulated external birds, they are less certain that the shadows are caused by external birds than they are that birdlike shadows do appear on the translucent walls of the cubical world. Since the degree of probability is different for each of these statements, the claim that identical testable consequences implies equivalence of meaning is false.

The point of this discussion is that just because no empirical test can decide between these two different ways of talking (i.e., birdlike shadows on the walls vs. external birds casting shadows on the walls), one must not conclude that these two ways of talking are cognitively equivalent. As Putnam puts it, Reichenbach understood that "sameness of testable consequences is not a good criterion for [cognitive] equivalence."[10] Thus, in showing himself able "to recognize differences in cognitive meaning between theories with the same testable consequences,"[11] Reichenbach showed himself to be less vulgar than other verificationists.

Why, then, does Reichenbach inconsistently fail to apply this same analysis to the case of the cat worshipper, which is identical to the case of the cubical world in comparing two cognitively different theories with the same testable consequences? Reverting to the most stringent form of verificationism, Reichenbach characterizes the difference in meaning between the testably equivalent statements in the case of the cat worshippers as a spurious transcendental meaning[12] (though Putnam points out that the acceptance by the cat worshippers of the cognitive equivalence of "Cats are divine animals" and "Cats inspire feelings of awe in cat worshippers" would have immediate relevance for their behavior[13]). This inconsistency, which Putnam calls "both bad semantics and bad philosophy"[14] is, perhaps, evidence that opposition to metaphysics—which is much more clearly involved in the case of the cat-worshippers than in the case of the cubical world—proved stronger for Reichenbach than consistent application of the very principle that he used to criticize the stringent identification of meaning with testable consequences in early verificationism.

Putnam's explication of Reichenbach's inconsistency on this point has important implications for theology: Even if it were the case (and I don't think it is) that a religious theory of life and a positivist theory of life were testably equivalent, it would be wrong to say that they are cognitively equivalent. For instance A. J. Ayer in his 1972-73 Gifford Lectures observed that a too stringent verification principle can lead to the unexpected consequence of accepting a proposition on the basis of propositions that (in Ayer's view) don't in fact support it. For example, one may take one's having prayed for rain and observed subsequently that it rained as evidence for the proposition that God exists. One who holds a stringent version of the verification principle could invoke the principle of equivalence at this point and assert that what one means by claiming that God exists is that one sometimes gets what one prays for.[15]

This is a neat trick, but it cuts two ways. For the committed theist may respond by asking if all one means by claiming that God doesn't exist is that sometimes one doesn't get what one prays for? If so, this is a jejune and self-centered way of conceiving God. For the devout person, whose faith has transcended the commercial *do ut des* relationship with God, the outcome of prayer for things like rain and so forth has no bearing on her belief that God exists. As can be seen in traditional piety, a radical distinction is made between the belief in the existence of God and the attempt to select some events in life as verifying consequences of that belief. This attitude is eloquently expressed by Job when he exclaims, in the midst of almost unendurable misfortune, "though he slay me, yet will I hope in him . . ." (Job 13:15a [New International Version]). This nonmanipulative, noncommercial piety seeks no special favors from God and thus effectively cuts the link between cognitive equivalence of meaning and identity of testable consequences. Although the devout believer experiences the same consequences as the unbeliever—illness, loss, grief, and death—the profoundly faithful person refuses to take these events as evidence for the proposition that God does not exist. Another example, chosen almost at random from traditional Christian devotional writings, eloquently exemplifies the lack of self-concern, which characterizes true and radical belief in God:

> Lord, I will suffer willingly for thee whatsoever Thou art pleased should befall me. I will receive with indifference from Thy hand good and evil, sweet and bitter, joy and sorrow, and will give Thee thanks for all that happens to me.[16]

It is clear, then, that the principle of equivalence is incapable of exhausting the meaning of what the believer means by the claim that God exists, and, consequently, the stringent verificationist assault upon theology is ineffective.

Notes

[1] Hilary Putnam, *Realism and Reason* (New York: Cambridge University Press, 1983), 27; *Meaning and the Moral Sciences* (Boston: Routledge & Kegan Paul, 1978), 18, 265. However, R. W. Ashby observes that "Moritz Schlick and other logical positivists sometimes said that the meaning of a sentence is the method of its verification. But unlike the advocates of operationalism [including P. W. Bridgman], they meant by 'the method of verification' not an actual procedure but the logical possibility of verification" (*The Encyclopedia of Philosophy*, s.v. "verifiability principle"). Putnam distinguishes between verificationism and operationism in *Realism and Reason*, 266 note †.

[2] Putnam, *Realism and Reason*, 27, 29.

[3] Putnam, following Hans Reichenbach, points out that it is a crude positivism (sometimes called 'operationism') that trusts in *logically necessary* equivalences to establish the meaning of concepts. For the statement "Current is flowing in the wire if and only if the voltmeter needle is deflected," is only approximately true (*Realism and Reason*, 27). For instance, there may be some mechanical problem with the voltmeter. Current flowing through a defective voltmeter might not displace the needle. Thus, there is more to the defining of the term *current* than mere reference to the behavior of a voltmeter needle (*Realism and Reason*, 27). This would seem to outlaw the use of the logical operator ≡ , since it implies necessity. It is precisely this difference that will eventually help to distinguish the vulgar forms of early verificationism from later, more subtle ones.

[4] Ibid., 30.

[5] Ibid., 27.

[6] Putnam, *Realism and Reason*, 29-30. See also Hans Reichenbach, *Experience and Prediction: An Analysis of the Foundations and the Structure of Knowledge* (Chicago: The University of Chicago Press, 1938), 66-68.

[7] Putnam, *Realism and Reason*, 28.

[8] Ibid., 29. See also Reichenbach, *Experience and Prediction*, 115-35.

[9] Ibid., 29.

[10] Ibid., 29.

[11] Ibid., 30.

[12] Ibid., 30

[13] Hilary Putnam, *Reason, Truth, and History* (New York: Cambridge University Press, 1981), 112-13.

[14] Putnam, Realism and Reason, 30.

[15] A. J. Ayer, *The Central Questions of Philosophy* (London: Weidenfeld and Nicolson, 1973), 26.

[16] Thomas à Kempis, *My Imitation of Christ*, rev. ed. (Brooklyn: Confraternity of the Precious Blood, 1954), III. 17.4 (217).

Select Bibliography

Although extensive, the sections listing writings by and about John Hick are not complete. An exhaustive bibliography of Hick's writings up until 1986 may be found in Gavin D'Costa, *John Hick's Theology of Religions: A Critical Evaluation* (Lanham, MD: University Press of America, 1987).

1. John Hick

Books

Hick, John. *Faith and Knowledge: A Modern Introduction to the Problem of Religious Knowledge.* Ithaca: Cornell University Press, 1957.

————. *Philosophy of Religion.* 1st ed. Englewood Cliffs, NJ: Prentice-Hall, 1963.

————. *Faith and Knowledge.* 2d ed. 1966; reissue, London: Macmillan, 1988.

————. *Christianity at the Centre.* New York: Herder and Herder, 1970.

————. *Philosophy of Religion.* 2d ed. Englewood Cliffs, NJ: Prentice-Hall, 1973.

————. *Death and Eternal Life.* New York: Harper & Row, 1976.

————. *God and the Universe of Faiths.* Reissue of 2d 1977 edition. London: Macmillan, 1988.

————. *God Has Many Names.* London: Macmillan Press, 1980.

————. *God Has Many Names.* Philadelphia: The Westminster Press, 1982.

Goulder, Michael and John Hick. *Why Believe in God?* London: SCM Press, 1983.

Hick, John. *Problems of Religious Pluralism*. New York: Macmillan Press, 1985.

Hick, John and Lamont C. Hempel. *Gandhi's Significance for Today*. London: Macmillan, 1989.

Hick, John. *An Interpretation of Religion: Human Responses to the Transcendent*. New Haven: Yale University Press, 1989.

————. *Disputed Questions*. New Haven: Yale University Press, 1993.

————. *The Metaphor of God Incarnate: Christology in a Pluralistic Age*. Louisville, KY: Westminster/John Knox Press, 1993.

Articles

Some of the articles cited below have appeared in journals before appearing in volumes of collected articles edited by Hick and, in one case, Paul Badham. Rather than give the information on where the article first appeared, I have indicated in which volume of collected articles it appears. I do this because Hick often edited articles for republication and also because the pagination of these articles when quoted or cited in this book corresponds to the pagination of the edited volume. Original publication data can be found in prefaces, acknowledgments to the various volumes in which the articles were republished (or, in the case of *Problems of Religious Pluralism*, at the bottom of the first page of the chapter that constitutes the republished article, and, in the case of "Theology and Verification," in footnote one). For articles not in these volumes or that I consulted in their original setting, I have given the original publication information. Since Hick's works are being listed in chronological order, I have placed the year of original publication or presentation in brackets at the end of their respective entries.

Hick, John. "The Will to Believe: William James's Theory of Faith." *The London Quarterly and Holborn Review* 177 (1952): 290–95.

———. "Theology and Verification." In *The Existence of God*, edited by John Hick. New York: Macmillan, 1964 [1960]

———. "Comment" on Luther J. Binkley's "What Characterizes Religious Language." *Journal for the Scientific Study of Religion* 2 (1962): 22–24.

———. "A Comment on Professor Binkley's Reply." *Journal for the Scientific Study of Religion* 2 (1963): 231–32.

———. "Sceptics and Believers." In *Faith and the Philosophers*, edited by John Hick. London: Macmillan, 1964.

———. "Religion as Fact-asserting." In *A John Hick Reader*, edited by Paul Badham. Philadelphia: Trinity Press, 1990 [1968].

———. "The Reconstruction of Christian Belief." In *God and the Universe of Faiths*. Reissue of 2d. 1977 ed. London: Macmillan, 1988 [1970].

———. "The Copernican Revolution in Theology." In *God and the Universe of Faiths*. Reissue of 2d. 1977 ed. London: Macmillan, 1988 [1973].

———. "The Essence of Christianity." In *God and the Universe of Faiths*. Reissue of 2d. 1977 ed. London: Macmillan, 1988 [1973].

———. "The New Map of the Universe of Faiths." In *God and the Universe of Faiths*. Reissue of 2d. 1977 ed. London: Macmillan, 1988 [1973].

———. "Theology's Central Problem." In John Hick, *God and the Universe of Faiths*. Reissue of 2d. 1977 ed. London: Macmillan, 1988 [1973].

———. "By Whatever Path. . . ." *God Has Many Names*. Philadelphia: The Westminster Press, 1982 [1974].

———. "The Outcome: Dialogue into Truth." In *Truth and Dialogue in World Religions: Conflicting Truth-Claims*, edited by John Hick. Philadelphia: The Westminster Press, 1974.

———. "Whatever Path Men Choose is Mine." In *God Has Many Names*. London: Macmillan Press, 1980 [1974].

———. "Eschatological Verification Reconsidered." In *Problems of Religious Pluralism*. New York: Macmillan Press, 1985 [1977].

———. "Jesus and the World Religions." In *The Myth of God Incarnate*, edited by John Hick. Philadelphia: Westminster, 1977.

———. "Remarks." In *Reason and Religion*, edited by Stuart C. Brown. Ithaca: Cornell University Press, 1977.

———. "Present and Future Life." In *Problems of Religious Pluralism*. New York: Macmillan Press, 1985 [1978].

———. "On Grading Religions." *Religious Studies* 17 (1981): 451–67.

———. "Towards a Philosophy of Religious Pluralism." *God has Many Names*. Philadelphia: The Westminster Press, 1982.

———. "Christ in a Universe of Faiths." Leicester, UK: Quaker Universalist Group, 1983.

———. "In Defence of Religious Pluralism." In *Problems of Religious Pluralism*. New York: Macmillan Press, 1985 [1983].

———. "On Conflicting Religious Truth-Claims." *Religious Studies* 19 (1983): 485–91.

———. "The Theology of Religious Pluralism." *Theology* 86 (1983): 335–40.

———. "A Philosophy of Religious Pluralism." In *Problems of Religious Pluralism*. New York: Macmillan Press, 1985 [1984].

———. "Religious Pluralism and Absolute Claims." In *Problems of Religious Pluralism*. New York: Macmillan Press, 1985 [1984].

161

———. "Religious Diversity as Challenge and Promise." In *The Experience of Religious Diversity*, edited by John Hick and Hasan Askari. Brookfield, VT: Gower Publishing, 1985.

———. "Three Controversies." *Problems of Religious Pluralism*. New York: Macmillan Press, 1985.

———. "Religious Pluralism." *The Encyclopedia of Religion*. 1986.
———. "The Buddha's Undetermined Questions and the Conflicting Truth Claims of Different Religions." In *Hermeneutics, Religious Pluralism, and Truth*, edited by Gregory D. Pritchard. Winston-Salem, NC: Wake Forest University, 1989 [1987]. This article was reprinted as "The Buddha's Doctrine of the 'Undetermined Questions.'" In *Disputed Questions*, edited by John Hick. New Haven: Yale University Press, 1993.

———. "The Non-Absoluteness of Christianity." In *The Myth of Christian Uniqueness: Toward a Pluralistic Theology of Religions*, edited by John Hick and Paul F. Knitter. Maryknoll, NY: Orbis Books, 1987.

———. "An Inspiration Christology for a Religiously Plural World." In *Encountering Jesus*, edited by Stephen Davis. Philadelphia: Fortress Press, 1988.

———. "A Possible Conception of Life After Death." In *Death and Afterlife*, edited by Stephen T. Davis. New York: St. Martin's Press, 1989.

———. Response to Kai Nielsen's "The Faces of Immortality." In *Death and Afterlife*, edited by Stephen T. Davis. New York: St. Martin's Press, 1989.

———. "Trinity and Incarnation in the Light of Religious Pluralism." In *Three Faiths—One God: A Jewish, Christian, Muslim Encounter*, edited by John Hick and Edmund S. Meltzer. Albany: State University of New York Press, 1989.

———. "A Response to Gerald Loughlin." *Modern Theology* 7 (1990): 57–66.

———. "Straightening the Record: Some Response to Critics." *Modern Theology* 6 (1990): 187–95.

——. "Religion as 'Skillful Means': A Hint from Buddhism." *International Journal for Philosophy of Religion* (1991): 141–158.

——. "Religious Pluralism and the Rationality of Religious Belief." *Faith and Philosophy* 10 (1993): 242–49.

Edited Volumes

Hick, John, ed. *The Existence of God.* New York: Macmillan, 1964.

——, ed. *Faith and the Philosophers.* London: Macmillan, 1964.

——, ed. *Truth and Dialogue in World Religions: Conflicting Truth-Claims.* Philadelphia: The Westminster Press, 1974.

——, ed. *The Myth of God Incarnate.* Philadelphia: The Westminster Press, 1977.

Hick, John and Hasan Askari, eds. *The Experience of Religious Diversity.* Brookfield, VT: Gower Publishing, 1985.

Hick, John and Paul Knitter, eds. *The Myth of Christian Uniqueness: Toward a Pluralistic Theology of Religions.* Maryknoll, NY: Orbis Books, 1987.

Hick, John, ed. *Classical and Contemporary Readings in the Philosophy of Religion.* 3d ed. Englewood Cliffs, NJ: Prentice-Hall, 1990.

2. Writings All or in Part on John Hick

Almond, P. "John Hick's Copernican Revolution." *Theology* 86 (1983): 36–41.

Ariarajah, Wesley. *Hindus and Christians: A Century of Ecumenical Thought.* Grand Rapids, MI: William B. Eerdmans Publishing Company, 1991.

Apczynski. John V. "John Hick's Theocentrism: Revolutionary or Implicitly Exclusivist." *Modern* Theology 8 (1992): 39–52.

Audi, Robert. "Eschatological Verification and Personal Identity." *International Journal for Philosophy of Religion* 7 (1976): 392–408.

Badham, Paul. "The Philosophical Theology of John Hick." In *A John Hick Reader*, edited by Paul Badham. Philadelphia: Trinity Press International, 1990.

Binkley, Luther J. "Reply to Professor Hick's Comment on 'What Characterizes Religious Language.'" *Journal for the Scientific Study of Religion* 2 (1962): 18–22.

————. "What Characterizes Religious Language?" *Journal for the Scientific Study of Religion* 2 (1963): 228–30.

Brannigan, M. Review of *Problems of Religious Pluralism*, by John Hick. *Cross Currents* 36 (1986): 242–44.

Burrows, W. R. Review of *God Has Many Names*, by John Hick. *Cross Currents* 34 (1984): 232–35.

Byrne, P. "John Hick's Philosophy of Religion." *Scottish Journal of Theology* 35 (1982): 289–301.

Byrne, Peter. "A Religious Theory of Religion." *Religious Studies* 27 (1991): 121–32.

Campbell, James I. *The Language of Religion*. New York: The Bruce Publishing Company, 1971.

Carruthers, Gregory H. *The Uniqueness of Jesus in the Theocentric Model of the Christian Theology of Religions: An Elaboration and Evaluation of the Position of John Hick*. Lanham, MD: University Press of America, 1990.

Cell, Edward. *Language, Existence, and God*. Nashville: Abingdon Press, 1971.

Corliss, Richard L. "Redemption and the Divine Realities: A Study of Hick and an Alternative." *Religious Studies* 22 (1986): 235–48.

Craighead, Houston A. Review of *Problems of Religious Pluralism*, by John Hick. *The International Journal for the Philosophy of Religion* 25 (1989): 187–89.

Cupitt, Don. "Thin-Line Theism." Review of *God Has Many Names*, by John Hick. *Times Literary Supplement*, 8 August 1980.

Davis, Stephen T. "Theology, Verification, and Falsification," *International Journal for Philosophy of Religion* 6 (1975): 23–39.

———. *Faith, Scepticism, and Evidence: An Essay in Religious Epistemology*. Lewisburg, PA: Bucknell University Press, 1978.

———, ed. *Death and Afterlife*. New York: St. Martin's Press, 1989.

D'Costa, Gavin. *Theology and Religious Pluralism: The Challenge of Other Religions*. London: Basil Blackwell, 1986.

———. *John Hick's Theology of Religions: A Critical Evaluation*. Lanham, MD: University Press of America, 1987.

D'Costa, Gavin. "John Hick's Copernican Revolution: Ten Years After." *New Blackfriars* 65 (1984): 323–31.

———."An Answer to Mr Loughlin." *New Blackfriars* 46 (1985): 135–37.

———. "Elephants, Ropes and a Christian Theology of Religions." *Theology* 87 (1985): 259–68.

———. "The Pluralist Paradigm in the Christian Theology of Religions." *Scottish Journal of Theology* 39 (1986): 211–24.

———. *Theology and Religious Pluralism: The Challenge of Other Religions*. Oxford: Basil Blackwell, 1986.

———. Review of *The Metaphor of God Incarnate*, by John Hick. *Religious Studies* 31 (1995): 136–38.

Donovan, Peter. *Religious Language*. New York: Hawthorn Books, 1976.

Edwards, Rem B. *Reason and Religion: An Introduction to the Philosophy of Religion*. New York: Harcourt Brace Jovanovich, 1972.

Forgie, William J. "Hyper-Kantianism in Recent Discussions of Mystical Experience." *Religious Studies* 21 (1985): 205–18.

Forrester, Duncan B. "Professor Hick and the Universe of Faiths." *Scottish Journal of Theology* 29 (1976): 65–72.

Gillis, Chester. *A Question of Final Belief: John Hick's Pluralistic Theory of Salvation.* London: Macmillan Press, 1989.

———. Review of *An Interpretation of Religion: Human Responses to the Transcendent,* by John Hick. *The Journal of Religion* 70 (1990): 270–71.

Godlove, Terry F., Jr. *Religion, Interpretation, and Diversity of Belief: The Framework Model From Kant to Durkheim to Davidson.* New York: Cambridge University Press, 1989.

Griffiths, Paul and Lewis Delmas. "On Grading Religions, Seeking Truth, and Being Nice to People—A Reply to Professor Hick." *Religious Studies* 19 (1983): 75–80.

Grover, Stephen. "Unmatching Mysteries." Review of *An Interpretation of Religion: Human Responses to the Transcendent,* by John Hick. *Times Literary Supplement,* 22–28 December 1989.

Heim, S. Mark. "The Pluralistic Hypothesis, Realism, and Post-Eschatology." *Religious Studies* 28 (1992): 207–19.

Hewitt, Harold, Jr., ed. *Problems in the Philosophy of Religion: Critical Studies of the Work of John Hick.* New York: St. Martin's Press, 1991.

Hunt, Anne. "No Other Name? A Critique of Religious Pluralism." *Pacifica* 3 (1990): 45–60.

Jeffner, Anders. *The Study of Religious Language.* London: SCM Press, 1972.

Kaufman, Gordon D. "Religious Diversity and Religious Truth." In *God, Truth, and Reality: Essays in Honor of John Hick,* edited by Arvind Sharma. St. Martin's Press: New York, 1993.

Kavka, Gregory S. "Eschatological Falsification." *Religious Studies* 12 (1976): 201–05.

Kellenberger, J. *The Cognitivity of Religion: Three Perspectives.* Berkeley: University of California Press, 1985.

Kennick, W. E. Review of *Faith and Knowledge: A Modern Introduction to the Problem of Religious Knowledge*, by John Hick. *Philosophical Review* 57 (1958): 407–09.

Klein, Kenneth H. *Positivism and Christianity: A Study of Theism and Verifiability*. The Hague: Martinus Nijhoff, 1974.

Knitter, Paul. *No Other Name? A Critical Survey of Christian Attitudes Toward the World Religions*. Maryknoll, NY: Orbis Books, 1985.

Lipner, Julius. "Truth-Claims and Inter-Religious Dialogue." *Religious Studies* 12 (1976): 217–30.

————. J[ulius]. J. "Does Copernicus Help? Reflections for a Christian Theology of Religions." *Religious Studies* 13 (1977): 243–58.

————. Review of *Theo-monistic Mysticism: A Hindu-Christian Comparison*, by Michael Stoeber. *Religious Studies* 31 (1995): 140-41.

Loughlin, Gerard. "Paradigms and Paradox: Defending the Case for a Revolution in the Theology of Religions." *New Blackfriars* 66 (1985): 127–35.

————. "Noumenon and Phenomena." *Religious Studies* 23 (1987): 493–508.

————. "Prefacing Pluralism: John Hick and the Mastery of Religion." *Modern Theology* 7 (1990): 30–55.

Louw, Dirk J. "Theocentrism and Reality-centrism: A Critique of John Hick and Wilfred Cantwell Smith's Philosophy of Religion." *South African Journal of Philosophy* 13 (1994): 1–8.

Mackie, Beth. "Concerning 'Eschatological Verification Reconsidered.'" *Religious Studies* 23 (1987): 129–35.

Mathis, Terry Richard. *Against John Hick*. Boston: University Press of America, 1985.

Mavrodes, George I. "God and Verification." *Canadian Journal of Theology* 10 (1964): 187–91.

Mesle, C. Robert. Review of *An Interpretation of Religion: Human Responses to the Transcendent*, by John Hick. *Journal of the American Academy of Religion* 53 (1990): 710–14.

Min, Anselm K. "Christology and Theology of Religions: John Hick and Karl Rahner." *Louvain Studies* 11 (1986): 3–21.

Mitchell, Basil. *The Justification of Religious Belief.* London: Macmillan, 1973.

Nash, Ronald H. *Is Jesus the Only Savior?* Grand Rapids, MI: Zondervan Publishing House, 1994.

Netland, Harold A. *Dissonant Voices: Religious Pluralism and the Question of Truth.* Grand Rapids, MI: William B. Eerdmans Publishing Company, 1991.

———. "Professor Hick on Religious Pluralism." *Religious Studies* 22 (1986): 249–61.

Newbigin, Lesslie. *The Gospel in a Pluralist Society.* Grand Rapids, MI: William B. Eerdmans Publishing Co., 1989.

Nielsen, Kai. "Eschatological Verification." *Canadian Journal of Theology* 9 (1963): 271–81.

———. "Wittgensteinian Fideism." In *Contemporary Philosophy of Religion,* edited by Steven M. Cahn and David Shatz. New York: Oxford University Press, 1982 [1963].

———. "God and Verification Again." In *The Logic of God: Theology and Verificationism,* edited by Malcolm L. Diamond and Thomas V. Litzenburg, Jr. Indianapolis: The Bobbs-Merrill Company, 1975.

———. "Conceivability and Immortality: A Response to John Hick." In *Death and Afterlife,* edited by Stephen T. Davis. New York: St. Martin's Press, 1989.

O'Hear, Anthony. "The real or the Real? Chardin or Rothko?" *Philosophy* 32 (1992): 47–58.

Pannenberg, Wolfhart. "Constructive and Critical Functions of Christian Eschatology." *Harvard Theological Review* 77 (1984): 119–39.

Penelhum, Terence. *Religion and Rationality: An Introduction to the Philosophy of Religion.* New York: Random House, 1971.

Pinnock, Clark H. *A Wideness in God's Mercy: The Finality of Jesus Christ in a World of Religions.* Grand Rapids, MI: Zondervan Publishing House, 1992.

Price, H. H. *Belief.* New York: Humanities Press, 1969.

Race, Alan. *Christians and Religious Pluralism: Patterns in the Christian Theology of Religions.* Maryknoll, NY: Orbis Books, 1982.

Reese, William L. "Religious Seeing-As." *Religious Studies* 14 (1978): 73–87.

Sanders, John. *No Other Name: An Investigation into the Destiny of the Unevangelized.* Grand Rapids, MI: William B. Eerdmans Publishing Company, 1992.

Sharma, Arvind, ed. *God, Truth, and Reality: Essays in Honor of John Hick.* St. Martin's Press: New York, 1993.

———. *The Philosophy of Religion and Advaita Vedānta: A Comparative Study in Religion and Reason.* University Park, PA: The Pennsylvania State University Press, 1995.

Siddiqi, Muzammil H. "A Muslim Response to John Hick: Trinity and Incarnation in the Light of Religious Pluralism." In *Three Faiths—One God: A Jewish, Christian, Muslim Encounter,* edited by John Hick and Edmund S. Meltzer. Albany: State University of New York Press, 1989.

Sontag, Frederick. "Anselm and the Concept of God." *Scottish Journal of Theology* 35 (1982): 213–18.

Stenger, Mary A. "The Problem of Cross-cultural Criteria of Religious Truths." *Modern Theology* 3 (1987): 315–32.

Stetson, Brad. *Pluralism and Particularity in Religious Belief.* Westport, CT: Praeger, 1994.

Stoeber, Michael. "Constructivist Epistemologies of Mysticism: A Critique and a Revision." *Religious Studies* 28 (1992): 107–16.

Surin, Kenneth. "A Certain 'Politics of Speech': 'Religious Pluralism' in the Age of the McDonald's Hamburger." *Modern Theology* 7 (1990): 67–100.

———. "Towards a 'Materialist' Critique of 'Religious Pluralism': An Examination of the Discourse of John Hick and Wilfred Cantwell Smith." In *Religious Pluralism and Unbelief: Studies Critical and Comparative*, edited by Ian Hammet. New York: Routledge, 1990.

Tooley, Michael. "John Hick and the Concept of Eschatological Verification." *Religious Studies* 12 (1976): 177–99.

Verkamp, Bernard J. "Hick's Interpretation of Religious Pluralism." *International Journal for Philosophy of Religion* 30 (1991): 103–24.

Ward, Keith. *Religion and Revelation*. New York: Oxford University Press, 1994.

———. "Truth and the Diversity of Religions." *Religious Studies* 26 (1990): 1–18.

3. Other Works Consulted

Ahlstrom, Sidney E. *A Religious History of the American People*. New Haven: Yale University Press, 1972.

Aldrich, Virgil C. "Messrs. Schlick and Ayer on Immortality." In *Readings in Philosophical Analysis*, edited by Herbert Feigl and Wilfrid Sellars. New York: Appleton-Century-Crofts, 1949.

Allison, Henry E. *Kant's Transcendental Idealism: An Interpretation and Defense*. New Haven: Yale University Press, 1983.

Aristotle. *Posterior Analytics*.

Ashby, R. W. "Verifiability Principle." *The Encyclopedia of Philosophy*.

Aune, Bruce. "Possibility." *The Encyclopedia of Philosophy*.

Ayer, A. J. *Language Truth and Logic*. 2d ed. 1946. Reprint. New York: Dover Publications, 1952.

––––––. *The Central Questions of Philosophy*. London: Weidenfeld and Nicolson, 1973.

––––––. *Philosophy in the Twentieth Century*. New York: Vintage Books, 1984.

––––––. *Wittgenstein*. Chicago: University of Chicago Press, 1986.

––––––, ed. *Logical Positivism*. New York: The Free Press, 1959.

Bagger, Matthew C. "Ecumenicalism and Perennialism Revisited." *Religious Studies* 27 (1991): 399–11.

Bennett, Jonathan. *Kant's Analytic*. Cambridge: Cambridge University Press, 1966.

––––––. *Kant's Dialectic*. Cambridge: Cambridge University Press, 1974.

Boyd, Robin. "A Barthian Theology of Interfaith Dialogue." *Pacifica* 3 (1990): 288–03.

Braithwaite, R. B. "An Empiricist's View of the Nature of Religious Belief." In *The Existence of God*, edited by John Hick. New York: Macmillan, 1964.

Brunner, Emil and Karl Barth. *Natural Theology*. Translated by Peter Fraenkel. London: Geoffrey Bles: The Centenary Press, 1946.

Burrell, David B. *Knowing the Unknowable God: Ibn-Sina, Maimonides, Aquinas*. Notre Dame: University of Notre Dame Press, 1986.

Carnap, Rudolf. *Pseudoproblems in Philosophy*. Translated by Rolf A. George. Berkeley: University of California Press, 1967.

––––––. "Testability and Meaning." In *Readings in the Philosophy of Science*, edited by Herbert Feigl and May Brodbeck. New York: Appleton-Century-Crofts, 1953.

Cavell, Stanley. *The Claim of Reason: Wittgenstein, Skepticism, Morality, and Tragedy.* New York: Oxford University Press, 1979.

Conant, James. "Introduction." In Hilary Putnam, *Realism with a Human Face,* edited by James Conant. Cambridge: Harvard University Press, 1990.

Crombie, I. M. "Theology and Falsification." In *New Essays in Philosophical Theology,* edited by Antony Flew and Alisdair MacIntyre. London: SCM Press, 1955.

Cutsinger, James S. Review of *The Essential Writings of Fritjhof Schuon,* edited by Seyyed Hossein Nasr. *Journal of the American Academy of Religion* 56 (1989): 209–213.

Deikman, Arthur J. "Deautomatization and the Mystic Experience." In *Understanding Mysticism,* edited by Richard Woods. Garden City, NY: Doubleday, 1980.

Dewey, John. *A Common Faith.* New Haven: Yale University Press, 1934.

Diamond, Malcolm L. "The Challenge of Contemporary Empiricism." In *The Logic of God: Theology and Verificationism,* edited by Malcolm L. Diamond and Thomas V. Litzenburg. Indianapolis: The Bobbs-Merrill Company, 1975

Diamond, Malcolm L. and Thomas V. Litzenburg, Jr. *The Logic of God: Theology and Verificationism.* Indianapolis: The Bobbs-Merrill Company, 1975.

Dionysius the Areopagite. *The Divine Names and The Mystical Theology.* 2d ed. Translated by C. E. Rolt. London: SPCK, 1940.

Feigl, Herbert. "Some Major Issues and Developments in the Philosophy of Science of Logical Empiricism." In *Minnesota Studies in the Philosophy of Science.* Vol. 1, *The Foundations of Science and the Concepts of Psychology and Psychoanalysis,* edited by Herbert Feigl and Michael Scriven. Minneapolis: Minnesota University Press, 1956.

Feigl, Herbert and Wilfrid Sellars, eds. *Readings in Philosophical Analysis.* New York: Appleton-Century-Crofts, 1949.

Feigl, Herbert and May Brodbeck, eds. *Readings in the Philosophy of Science*. New York: Appleton-Century-Crofts, 1953.

Ferré, Frederick. *Language, Logic, and God*. New York: Harper and Row, 1969.

―――. "Analogy in Theology." *The Encyclopedia of Philosophy*.

Findlay, J. N. *Kant and the Transcendental Object: A Hermeneutic Study*. New York: Oxford University Press, 1981.

Fiorenza, Francis Schüssler. *Foundational Theology: Theology and the Church*. New York: Crossroad, 1984.

Flew, Antony, R. M. Hare, Basil Mitchell, and I. M. Crombie. "Theology and Falsification." In *New Essays in Philosophical Theology*, edited by Antony Flew and Alisdair MacIntyre. London: SCM Press, 1955.

Forman, Robert K. C. "Paramartha and Modern Constructivists on Mysticism: Epistemological Monomorphism versus Duomorphism." *Philosophy East and West* 39 (1989): 393–18.

―――. "Introduction: Mysticism, Constructivism, and Forgetting." In *The Problem of Pure Consciousness: Mysticism and Philosophy*, edited by Robert K. C. Forman. New York: Oxford University Press, 1990.

―――, ed. *The Problem of Pure Consciousness: Mysticism and Philosophy*. New York: Oxford University Press, 1990.

Freeman, Kathleen. *Ancilla to the Pre-Socratic Philosophers: A Complete Translation of the Fragments in Diels, Fragmente der Vorsokratiker*. Cambridge: Harvard University Press, 1957.

Gandhi, M. K. *All Religions are True*. Edited by Anand T. Hingorani. Bombay: Bharatiya Vidya Bhavan, 1962.

Geertz, Clifford. *The Interpretation of Cultures: Selected Essays*. New York: Basic Books, 1973.

Gilson, Étienne. *The Unity of Philosophical Experience*. New York: Charles Scribner's Sons, 1937.

Goleman, Daniel and Robert A. F. Thurman, eds. *MindScience: An East-West Dialogue*. Boston: Wisdom Publications, 1991.

Gram, M. S. "How to Dispense with Things in Themselves (I)." *Ratio* 18 (1976): 1–16.

Grimes, John. *A Concise Dictionary of Indian Philosophy: Sanskrit Terms Defined in English*. Albany: State University of New York Press, 1989.

Guénon, René. *The Multiple States of Being*. Translated by J. Godwin. Burdett, NY: Larson, 1984.

Guignon, Charles. "Philosophy after Wittgenstein and Heidegger." *Philosophy and Phenomenological Research* 50 (1990): 649–672.

Habermas, Gary and Antony Flew. *Did Jesus Rise from the Dead? The Resurrection Debate*. Edited by Terry L. Miethe. San Francisco: Harper and Row, 1987.

Hanfling, Oswald. *Logical Positivism*. New York: Columbia University Press, 1981.

———. "Introduction." In *Essential Readings on Logical Positivism*, edited by Oswald Hanfling. Oxford: Basil Blackwell, 1981.

Hepburn, Ronald W. *Christianity and Paradox: Critical Studies in Twentieth-Century Theology*. London: Watts, 1958.

Hirst, R. J. "Realism." *The Encyclopedia of Philosophy*.

Horwich, Paul. *Truth*. Cambridge, MA: Basil Blackwell, 1990.

Hughes, Christopher. *On a Complex Theory of a Simple God: An Investigation in Aquinas' Philosophical Theology*. Ithaca: Cornell University Press, 1989.

Incandela, Joseph M. "The Appropriation of Wittgenstein's Work by Philosophers of Religion: Towards a Re-evaluation and an End." *Religious Studies* 21 (1985): 457–74.

James, William. "The Will to Believe." In *The Will to Believe and Other Essays on Popular Philosophy*. 1896; reprint, New York: Dover Publications, 1956.

Jelly, Frederick M. "The Relationship Between Symbolic and Literary Language about God." In *Naming God*, edited by Robert P. Scharlemann. New York: Paragon House, 1985.

Kant, Immanuel. *Critique of Pure Reason*. Translated by Norman Kemp Smith. New York: St. Martin's Press, 1965.

—————. *Critique of Practical Reason*. Translated by Lewis White Beck. Indianapolis: Bobbs-Merrill Company, 1956.

—————. *Religion within the Bounds of Reason Alone*. Translated by Theodore M. Greene and Hoyt H. Hudson. 2d ed. New York: Harper and Row, 1960.

Katz, Steven T. "Language, Epistemology, and Mysticism." In *Mysticism and Philosophical Analysis*, edited by Steven T. Katz. New York: Oxford University Press, 1978.

—————. "The 'Conservative' Character of Mysticism." In *Mysticism and Religious Traditions*, edited by Steven T. Katz. New York: Oxford University Press, 1983.

—————. "On Mysticism." *Journal of the American Academy of Religion* 56 (1988): 751–57.

—————, ed. *Mysticism and Philosophical Analysis*. New York: Oxford University Press, 1978.

—————, ed. *Mysticism and Religious Traditions*. New York: Oxford University Press, 1983.

Kaufman, Gordon D. *Relativism, Knowledge, and Faith*. Chicago: The University of Chicago Press, 1960.

—————. *God the Problem*. Cambridge: Harvard University Press, 1972.

—————. *An Essay on Theological Method*. Revised Edition. Missoula, Montana: Scholars Press, 1975.

—————. *The Theological Imagination: Constructing the Concept of God*. Philadelphia: The Westminster Press, 1981.

—————. *Theology for a Nuclear Age*. Philadelphia: The Westminster Press, 1985.

————. *In Face of Mystery: A Constructive Theology.* Cambridge: Harvard University Press, 1993.

————. "Mystery, Theology, and Conversation." *Harvard Divinity Bulletin* 21 (1991–92): 12–14.

Kerr, Fergus. *Theology after Wittgenstein.* Oxford: Basil Blackwell, 1986.

Kierkegaard, Søren Aabye. *Concluding Unscientific Postscript.* Translated by David F. Swenson and Walter Lowrie. Princeton: Princeton University Press, 1941.

King, Sallie B. "Two Epistemological Models for the Interpretation of Mysticism." *Journal of the American Academy of Religion* 56 (1988): 257–79.

————. Response to Steven T. Katz. *Journal of the American Academy of Religion* 56 (1988): 759–61.

Klubertanz, George P. *St. Thomas on Analogy: A Textual and Systematic Synthesis.* Chicago: Loyola University Press, 1960.

Kraemer, Hendrik. *The Christian Message in Non-Christian World.* 2d. ed. New York: International Missionary Council, 1946.

Kraft, Victor. *The Vienna Circle: The Origin of Neo-Positivism, A Chapter in the History of Recent Philosophy.* Translated by A. Pap. 1953; reprint, New York: Greenwood Press, 1969.

Küng, Hans, et al. *Christianity and the World Religions: Paths to Dialogue with Islam, Hinduism and Buddhism.* Translated by Peter Heinegg. New York: Doubleday, 1986.

Laughlin, Charles D., John McManus, and Eugene G. d'Aquili. *Brain, Symbol, and Experience: Toward a Neurophenomenology of Human Consciousness.* Boston: Shambhala, 1990.

Lindbeck, George. *The Nature of Doctrine: Religion and Doctrine in a Postliberal Age.* Philadelphia: The Westminster Press, 1984.

Lyttkens, Hampus. *The Analogy between God and the World: An Investigation of Its Background and Interpretation of Its Use by Thomas of Aquino.* Uppsala: Almqvist & Wiksells Boktrycckeri AB, 1952.

176

The Māṇḍūkya Upaniṣad with Gauḍapāda's and Śaṅkara's Commentary. 5th ed. Translated by Swami Nikhilananda. Calcutta: Advaita Ashrama, 1987.

Marsden, George. *Fundamentalism and American Culture: The Shaping of Twentieth-Century Evangelicalism 1870–1925.* New York: Oxford University Press, 1980.

Marty, Martin E. and R. Scott Appleby, eds. *Fundamentalisms Observed.* Chicago: University of Chicago Press, 1991.

McCabe, Herbert. Commentary and Translation. Thomas Aquinas, *Summa Theologiae* Vol. 3, *Knowing and Naming God.* New York: Blackfriars/McGraw-Hill, 1964.

McDermott, Robert. "The Religion Game: Some Family Resemblances." *Journal of the American Academy of Religion* 38 (1970).

Mitchell, Basil. *Faith and Logic: Oxford Essays in Philosophical Theology.* London: George Allen & Unwin, 1957.

Monk, Ray. *Ludwig Wittgenstein: The Duty of Genius.* New York: The Free Press, 1990.

Moore, A. W. *The Infinite.* New York: Routledge, 1990.

Mtega, Norbert W. *Analogy and Theological Language in the Summa Contra Gentiles: A Textual Survey of the Concept of Analogy and Its Theological Application by St. Thomas.* Frankfurt am Main: Peter Lang, 1984.

Nasr, Seyyed Hossein. *Knowledge and the Sacred.* 1981; reprint, Albany: The State University Press of New York, 1989.

Needleman, Jacob, ed. *The Sword of Gnosis: Metaphysics, Cosmology, Tradition, Symbolism.* Baltimore: Penguin Books, 1974.

Niebuhr, H. Richard. Paperback Edition. *The Meaning of Revelation.* New York: Macmillan, 1960.

Passmore, John. *Recent Philosophers.* LaSalle, IL: Open Court Publishing Company, 1985.

Pelikan, Jaroslav. *The Christian Tradition: A History of the Development of Doctrine*. Vol. 2, *The Spirit of Eastern Christendom (600–1700)*. Chicago: University of Chicago Press, 1974.

Pereira, José, ed. *Hindu Theology: A Reader*. Garden City, NY: Image Books, 1976.

Plato. *Phaedo*.

———. *Republic*.

Preller, Victor. *Divine Science and the Science of God: A Reformulation of Thomas Aquinas*. Princeton: Princeton University Press, 1967.

Putnam, Hilary. *Meaning and the Moral Sciences*. Boston: Routledge & Kegan Paul, 1978.

———. *Reason, Truth, and History*. New York: Cambridge University Press, 1981.

———. *Realism and Reason*. Vol. 3, *Philosophical Papers*. Cambridge: Cambridge University Press, 1983.

———. *The Many Faces of Realism*. LaSalle, IL: Open Court Publishing Company, 1987.

———. *Realism with a Human Face*. Edited by James Conant. Cambridge: Harvard University Press, 1990.

———. *Renewing Philosophy*. Cambridge: Harvard University Press, 1992.

———. "Ultimate Questions." William James Lecture on Religious Experience at Harvard Divinity School. 1990 (unpublished).

Reichenbach, Hans. *Experience and Prediction: An Analysis of the Foundations and the Structure of Knowledge*. Chicago: The University of Chicago Press, 1938.

———. "The Verifiability Theory of Meaning." In *Readings in the Philosophy of Science*, edited by Herbert Feigl and May Brodbeck. New York: Appleton-Century-Crofts, 1953.

Rescher, Nicholas. *A Theory of Possibility: A Constructivistic and Conceptualistic Account of Possible Individuals and Possible Worlds*. Pittsburgh: University of Pittsburgh Press, 1975.

Rothberg, Donald. "Understanding Mysticism: Transpersonal Theory and the Limits of Contemporary Epistemological Frameworks." *Revision* 12 (1989): 5–21.

Schlick, Moritz. "Meaning and Verification." In *Readings in Philosophical Analysis*, edited by Herbert Feigl and Wilfrid Sellars. New York: Appleton-Century-Crofts, 1949.

Schuon, Frithjof. *The Transcendent Unity of Religions*. Revised edition. Wheaton, IL: Theosophical Publishing House, 1984.

Smith, Huston. *Forgotten Truth*. New York: Harper and Row, 1976.

———. "Is There a Perennial Philosophy." *Journal of the American Academy of Religion* 55 (1987): 554–66.

———. Response to Steven T. Katz. *Journal of the American Academy of Religion* 56 (1988): 757–59.

Splett, Jörg and Lourencino Bruno Puntel. "Analogy of Being." *Sacramentum Mundi: An Encyclopedia of Theology*.

Stace, W. T. *Mysticism and Philosophy*. New York: J. B. Lippincott, 1960.

Swidler, Leonard. *After the Absolute: The Dialogical Future of Religious Reflection*. Minneapolis: Fortress Press, 1990.

Tallet, J. A. *The Possible Universe*. Publitex: Houston, 1990.

Thomas à Kempis. *My Imitation of Christ*. Revised Translation. Brooklyn: Confraternity of the Precious Blood, 1954.

Thomas Aquinas. *Summa Theologica*. Vol. 1, *Pars Prima et Prima Secundae*. Translated by the Fathers of the English Dominican Province. New York: Benziger Brothers, 1947.

———. *Summa Theologiae*. Vol. 3, *Knowing and Naming God*. Translated by Herbert McCabe. New York: Blackfriars/McGraw-Hill, 1964.

————. *Saint Thomas Aquinas: Philosophical Texts.* Translated by Thomas Gilby. New York: Oxford University Press, 1960.

Tillich, Paul. *Christianity and the Encounter of the World Religions.* New York: Columbia University Press, 1963.

Troeltsch, Ernst. "The Place of Christianity among the World Religions." In John Hick, ed., *Classical and Contemporary Readings in the Philosophy of Religion.* 3d ed., edited by John Hick. Englewood Cliffs, NJ: Prentice-Hall, 1990.

Urmson, J. O. *Philosophical Analysis: Its Development Between the Two World Wars.* London: Oxford University Press, 1956.

van Buren, Paul M. *The Edges of Language: An Essay in the Logic of a Religion.* New York: Macmillan, 1972.

Wieman, Henry Nelson. *Man's Ultimate Commitment.* Carbondale, IL: Southern Illinois University Press, 1958.

Wisdom, John. "Gods." In *Classical and Contemporary Readings in the Philosophy of Religion.* 3d ed., edited by John Hick. Englewood Cliffs, NJ: Prentice-Hall, 1990.

Wittgenstein, Ludwig. *Lectures and Conversations on Aesthetics, Psychology and Religious Belief.* Compiled from Notes by Yorick Smythies, Rush Rhees and James Taylor, and edited by Cyril Barrett. Berkeley: University of California Press, n.d.

————. *On Certainty.* Translated by Denis Paul and G. E. M. Anscombe. Oxford: Basil Blackwell, 1969.

Index

Toronto Studies in Religion

This series of monographs and books is designed as a contribution to the scholarly and academic understanding of religion. Such understanding is taken to involve both a descriptive and an explanatory task. The first task is conceived as one of surface description involving the gathering of information about religions, and depth description that provides, on the basis of the data gathered, a more finely nuanced description of a tradition's self-understanding. The second task concerns the search for explanation and the development of theory to account for religion and for particular historical traditions. The series will, furthermore, cover the phenomenon of religion in all its constituent dimensions and geographic diversity. Both established and younger scholars in the field will be included and will represent a wide range of viewpoints and positions, producing original work of high order at the monograph and major study level. Although predominantly empirically oriented, the series will also encourage theoretical studies and even leave room for creative and empirically controlled philosophical and speculative approaches in the interpretation of religions and religion. Toronto Studies in Religion will be of particular interest to those who study the subject at universities and colleges but will also be of value to the general educated reader.

DATE DUE

			Printed in USA

HIGHSMITH #45230